A synthesis of Antiquarian Observation and Archaeological Excavation at Dorchester-on-Thames, Oxfordshire

Wendy A. Morrison

BAR British Series 491
2009

Published in 2016 by
BAR Publishing, Oxford

BAR British Series 491

*A synthesis of Antiquarian Observation and Archaeological Excavation at Dorchester-on-Thames,
Oxfordshire*

ISBN 978 1 4073 0518 9

BAR Publishing is the trading name of British Archaeological Reports (Oxford) Ltd.
British Archaeological Reports was first incorporated in 1974 to publish the BAR
Series, International and British. In 1992 Hadrian Books Ltd became part of the BAR
group. This volume was originally published by Archaeopress in conjunction with
British Archaeological Reports (Oxford) Ltd / Hadrian Books Ltd, the Series principal
publisher, in 2009. This present volume is published by BAR Publishing, 2016.

Printed in England

BAR
PUBLISHING

BAR titles are available from:

BAR Publishing
122 Banbury Rd, Oxford, OX2 7BP, UK
EMAIL   info@barpublishing.com
PHONE   +44 (0)1865 310431
FAX   +44 (0)1865 316916
www.barpublishing.com

Table of Contents

Table of Figures

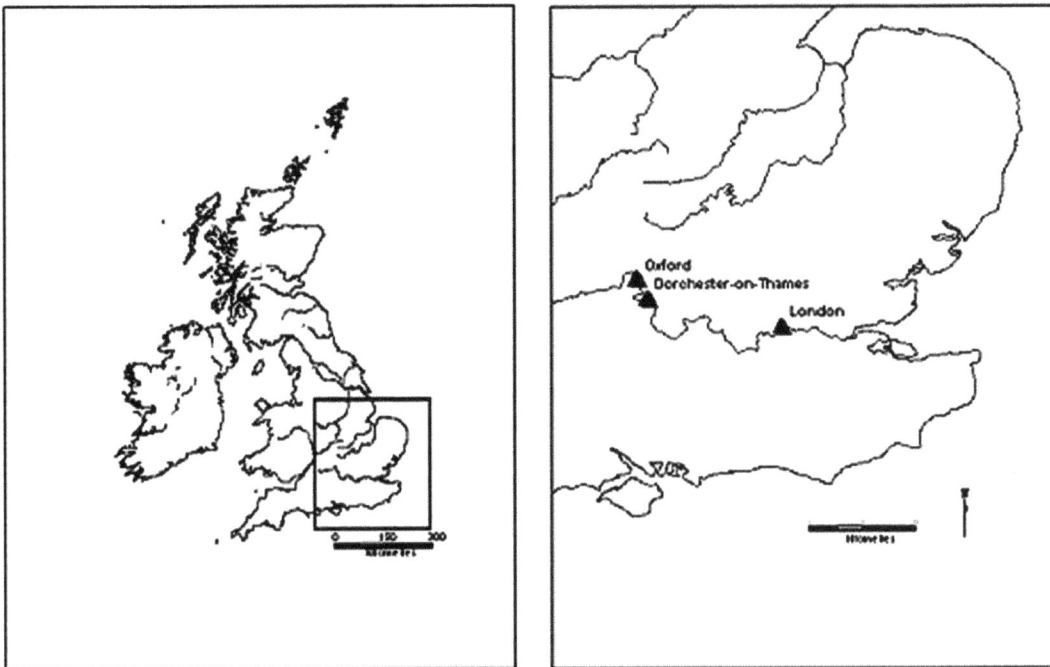

Figure 1. Location of Dorchester-on-Thames (SU 5794) in relation to southern England

Figure 2. Detail of Dorchester and environs
(Reproduced from Ordnance Survey map data by permission of Ordnance Survey, © Crown copyright)

PREFACE

This book was born out of research conducted in pursuit of a Master of Philosophy degree from the School of Archaeology, University of Oxford between 2006 and 2008.

Acknowledgements

I am indebted to a number of people for their assistance in the research carried out for this book. Thanks go to Professor Chris Gosden for his supervision during the thesis from which the book grew, as well as for introducing me to Dorchester-on-Thames, to Professor Sir Barry Cunliffe for his enthusiastic support and guidance, and to Ian Cartwright for photographic assistance and Dr Martin Henig for his comments on finds. I also extend gratitude to the museum staff who helped me to rifle through their archives in search of elusive excavation reports, specifically Dr. Alison Roberts of the Ashmolean Museum, Dr. Esther Cameron and Lydia Carr of the Oxfordshire County Museum Service, and John Metcalfe and Karen Selway-Richards of the Dorchester Abbey Museum, as well as Leigh Allen and Nick Shepherd of Oxford Archaeology who facilitated access to unpublished reports and to the finds. Particular thanks go to Professor Sheppard Frere and Professor Richard Bradley for taking the time to share their personal recollections of fieldwork undertaken. Paul Booth not only took time to read a draft of this work, but also to provide many helpful comments during all stages of writing. I am extremely grateful to Robin Bashford for all his help during the excavations at Dorchester and indeed for teaching me all I know about fieldwork. I thank Stacey McGowan for proofreading the drafts of this work, although any errors are completely my own. I thank all those among my friends who, with their boundless enthusiasm, have encouraged me in my work. Finally and most specially, I thank my husband John and our four children for their constant support and sacrifice during the research and writing process.

Chapter One

INTRODUCTION

"It is very rarely that one generation sweeps away the boundaries of its predecessors — rather they are preserved like scar-tissue embedded in the city's growth."(Cunliffe, 1986)

The sleepy village of Dorchester-on-Thames, with its thatched roofs and rose-clad cottages, might be one of a hundred 'biscuit-tin lid' villages, a place with an appearance, it has been written, that "neither invites attention nor excites interest" (Parker 1882, 49). Yet it is precisely the place that for over a century has indeed excited the interest of antiquarians and archaeologists because of its unrelenting position in the story of human settlement and occupation of the Thames Valley. In fact, the curiously enigmatic aspects of Dorchester's past have earned it a place of importance in almost any discussion of the late prehistory and early history of the Thames Valley (Henig and Booth 2003; Booth *et al* 2007; Benson and Miles 1974) or of the nation (Frere 1967; Burnham and Wacher 1990). Because of this academic interest, a few gems of knowledge about Dorchester have become fossilised in the narrative of the region, often to the point where they are often simply regurgitated in print, with little thought as to a modern re-evaluation of their origins or a deconstruction of the theories they have engendered. The last major research-led excavation in Dorchester was nearly half a century ago (Frere 1962; 1984) and although there have been subsequent publications of developer-driven excatavtions (Bradley 1978; Rowley and Brown 1974;) there has been "no recent synthesis of the development of Dorchester" (Oxford Archaeology 2007, 3) that takes into account all of the minor work that has gone on in the village, nor has that new information been placed within the re-examined context of the earlier publications.

Because Dorchester has exhibited evidence of human activity from at least the Neolithic period to the present with little apparent hiatus in occupation, the area has caused much the scholarly ink to flow over the past 150 years, from the collection of observations put together by Parker (1882) to the more professional offerings of Atkinson (1959) and Frere (1962; 1984), as well as an assortment of journal articles and entries which each offer a piecemeal look at the archaeology of the region. The last major synthesis of Dorchester was a small monograph published in 1985 (Cook and Rowley) that provided a wide audience with a sense of Dorchester's role in history but did little to open up greater academic discourse on the implications of that role.

More recently, an unpublished BA dissertation (Denning 2000) attempted to examine the evidence for settlement continuity over the millennia at Dorchester. Regrettably, it brought little to the discussion table, serving more as a gazetteer of published facts that raised the same questions, without postulating any answers. Warwick Rodwell's (2005) as yet unpublished work, *The Abbey Church of St Peter and St Paul,* provides a good cursory overview of the early antiquarian involvement in Dorchester and the general back-story of the village, but as his title implies, the bulk of the work is concerned with detailing the history of the medieval abbey and its environs, a task it accomplishes so well that it is considered unnecessary in these pages to venture very far into the realm of that building and its period.

The overarching theme running through most discussions of Dorchester is that of continuity, generally in reference to the apparent evidence for persistence of urban existence in the Late Roman - Early Medieval period. The town has become a focal point for the larger national debate over the nature of settlement and society in fifth and sixth century Britain. But the continuity perhaps represented at Dorchester may indeed span a greater period, from at least the Middle Iron Age to the Early Medieval. This is not a continuity of urban function, but a pervasiveness of core identity, an identity imbued by the shape of the landscape and the generations of lives lived upon it, that despite modifications and hybridisations retained an innate sense of self that weathered a storm comprised of wave after wave of external influences breaking upon an inherently stable population.

We have begun to abandon the invasionist views of the past, and no longer see the post-Roman continental invaders conducting a wholesale obliteration of the indigenous people (Higham 2004; Russell 2005). Also, we are questioning the nature of the Roman conquest, at least with regard to the southeastern Britain (Henig 2002; Creighton 2006). The very *fact* of Romanisation has gone under the knife and is emerging as something much more complex and fascinating (Millett 1990; Hingley 2003; Mattingly 2006). The role that landscape may play in the formation and preservation of identity has been opened up for exploration (Petts 1998) as well as how that geo-spatially determined sense of identity may have a genealogy of its own (Gosden and Lock 1998).

Thus it would seem that the time was ripe for a more inclusive and complete synthesis of the archaeology at Dorchester-on-Thames. This book attempts not only to fill the current void, but also to do more than simply collect all the existing information into one location. Rather, this is an attempt to look at a very significant place in new ways, with respect to the more traditional theoretical framework but not constrained by it. The result is a history of Dorchester in an overlapping double vision. One image presents the more traditionally understood place that Dorchester holds as the *oppidum* that grew up to be a town and retained that urban identity in the face of the crumbling fifth century, while the alternate hypothesis challenges the notion of 'urban' continuity, suggesting that stability of geographical presence and perseverance of spatial identity are more considerable factors in the longevity of Dorchester's significance.

Methodology

The methodology employed during the research for the production of this book was three-pronged in its approach. Firstly, it includes the often-overlooked contribution of antiquarian observers in centuries prior to the establishment of archaeology as an organised science. These learned individuals were perhaps in some ways misguided in their techniques and interpretations, yet none can deny that their passion for discovery and desire to understand the ancient world served to engender the more scientific application of archaeology in our own times. These early observers recorded what they saw with their own eyes, a century before the landscape was riddled with quarries, bypasses and housing estates. In an age before computerised databases, they kept careful collections of artefacts and began some of the first typologies. Perhaps most importantly, they disseminated their findings and their enthusiasm amongst other learned men in order to heighten awareness of the national importance of Britain's archaeology and to take measures to ensure its conservation and protection. Thus, this thesis incorporates antiquarian observations into the archaeological narrative of Dorchester, although those contributions will necessarily be viewed through the filter of modern understanding.

Secondly, this book seeks to re-evaluate previous excavations of the twentieth century in light of the changes in archaeological approaches, new theories, and interpretations that have come about during the intervening years. This required the examination of the archived records of excavations and where possible, personal interviews with the original excavators. Because of the quantity of information available concerning Roman Dorchester, this paper is necessarily more heavily weighted to that period. By delving more deeply into the records of excavation, rather than relying on the final publications, it is hoped that those fossilised *factoids* can be critically examined at the basic level and to see if they can stand the test of time, or if they require modification in light of new evidence. It should be clearly noted that no lack of respect is intended towards those individuals who laboured to illuminate Dorchester's past; it is simply good practice to review the current state of knowledge with regard to more recent views.

The third prong of the research methodology involved consultation of the growing body of "grey literature". This vast resource of new material, generated by the immense quantity of developer-driven archaeology, is often untapped by academic research, a trend that is slowly changing thanks to a few pioneering efforts (Bradley 2007; Yates 2007). Buried in museum archives, HERs (formerly SMRs) and the central files of commercial units, these unpublished reports, watching briefs and assessments can be rather difficult to access, but may contain vital information that affects the interpretation of a region. Often small in scale, these reports, when stitched together and viewed cumulatively over the area in question add to the archaeological tapestry that tells Dorchester's story. It would, however be remiss to ignore the fact that the practices of developer-driven field work, fuelled by the exigencies of financially motivated deadlines and internecine competition, may on occasion be less thorough or accurate than one might find desirable. Nonetheless, since the introduction of *Planning Policy Guidance 16: Archaeology and Planning* (PPG16) in 1990, Britain has experienced an incredible outburst of excavation, creating a resource that, when taken with a measure of caution, may radically change the current understanding of this island's past.

Caution is called for when utilising the grey literature reports for several reasons. The practice of tendering for developer funded archaeological evaluations and excavation has had the unfortunate knock-on effect of bringing 'lowest bidder' mentality to the arena. Although most commercial units strive to produce quality results and competent reporting within the budgetary constraints, there is always the danger that the quality of work had suffered under the pressure of time and funding. Additionally, although there is a codified set of standard set in place by the Institute for Archaeologists (IfA), there is no real mechanism in place to enforce the quality of the work conducted. The professional doctor or barrister must adhere to standards or risk malpractice complaints: there are no such measures regulating the work of archaeologists.[1] Nonetheless, if one is aware of these issues, and the possible effect they can have on the accuracy of the records and interpretations offered, an examination the unpublished commercial reports can indeed be of great use in piecing together the story of a region.

By combining these three sources of information, it is hoped that a new, up-dated, and challenging view of Dorchester is formed. The following chapters tell two interwoven narratives: that of the human occupation of this incredibly small yet significant place, and that of the journey of discovery taken by generations of antiquarians and archaeologists in their quest to reveal what that significance means. By laying all of the cards out on the academic table, we can then see exactly what we know, what we thought we knew, and what we want to know. A new research project began to unfold in Dorchester in 2007, with a view to intensify over the next five to ten years. Faced with a cornucopia of questions that need to be answered and such a wide range of periods to investigate, the directors of this project may be spoiled for choice. This book concludes with a few suggestions for areas that would benefit from attention in the future. As the following pages show, Dorchester has had an important relationship with archaeology for a long time, and one can see that the relationship must continue into the future.

---

[1] In fairness, it should be stated that the majority of the reports and records reviewed for this book were of very good quality and thoroughness, with only a few exceptions.

Chapter Two

EARLY PREHISTORY

"The larger issue of the importance of 'place' can never be quantified, but might be expected to be echoed through time.."(Loveday, 1999)

Geology

Positioned at the confluence of the Thames River and the south flowing Thame, Dorchester on Thames is nestled on a peninsular of land surrounded on three sides by water (Figure 1). The natural subsoil is the gravel terrace, part of the Summertown-Radley terrace (Benson and Miles 1974, 4). Faunal remains from this terrace indicate that the Palaeolithic saw intervals of both "cold" animals, such as mammoth and woolly rhinoceros, and "warm" animals including hippopotamus and a small species of elephant (Roe 1981, 122). Occasionally, evidence of human existence has surfaced in the form of microliths, flints and stone tools, but although several finds of Palaeolithic date are provenenced from the Dorchester region, the Mesolithic is rather poorly represented, indeed appearing barren on a distribution map for the period (Briggs *et al* 1986, 173). This apparent void in the evidence for human activity may be the result of patchy excavation and recovery of artefacts during development, or it may be a true indication of the abandonment of the region for a long period of time, perhaps influenced by changing patterns in animal populations and herd migration patterns. It is not exactly clear when precisely "the foragers became farmers" (Barker 2006), and the picture becomes considerably blurrier when one realises that there was likely an overlap between the use of metals and the continuance of a Neolithic way of life. Although pollen evidence exists for cereal cultivation in the area during the Late Bronze Age, evidence for earlier occupation is absent and the extent of any permanent settlement is uncertain (Hey 2007, 160).

Although assumed often that the light, free-draining soils of the gravel terraces and a relatively thin distribution of trees made the terraces highly attractive to early farmers, there appears to be little evidence to suggest that the tree cover was thin, and it is probable that the terraces were capable of sustaining substantial forests (Limbrey 1975, 192). The soils developing under this tree cover may have been greatly different from the regional soils at present, based upon the varying effects of the trees. Frustratingly, the body of pollen evidence for the Thames Valley is not as extensive as one might wish, permitting "only limited evidence on which to base a reconstruction of the natural vegetation cover" (Miles 1986, 20). If the area was indeed under dense forest, then the first true footprint of humans upon the landscape appears have been in the mid to late Neolithic, when "extensive tracts of cleared land were created in the river gravels" (Barclay and Hey 1999, 70).

Ironically, the very gravels that comprise the geology of the region and made the area so attractive for human development and settlement are the same gravels that imperil the traces of that long ago activity. The gravels located along the Thames have been exploited for millennia and there is evidence within the Dorchester settlement of gravel extraction pits dating from Roman and medieval contexts. Regrettably, the abundance of this gravel around Dorchester, which in strict preservation terms is ideal for the archaeological materials contained within, have perversely contributed to its wholesale destruction over the past few centuries. In 1735, an Act of Parliament gave permission for the extraction of gravel for the construction and improvement of Oxfordshire roads, proclaiming that any person could " dig, gather, take or carry away any gravel, sand, stones or other materials out of …any Common grounds in any village...without paying anything for such gravel" (Henley 1735, 236). This sparked a 'gravel rush' that saw the fields and wastes of the Dorchester Hundred exploited heavily, a trend that was to increase as technology advanced to allow the stripping of five tons of gravel in a single pass of the equipment (Benson and Miles 1974, 77).

Figure 3. Dorchester area cropmarks before (left) and after quarrying and by-pass construction (after Whittle et al *1992)*

By the 1930s, extraction companies were well on their way to obliterating the ancient features in the landscape. The fertility of the soils on this gravel terrace combined with excellent drainage created in the topsoil ideal conditions for the identification of cropmarks (Figure 3), and indeed after the debut of aerial reconnaissance in the First World War, the Oxfordshire region was fortunate enough to be well documented in this way by several enthusiasts. The most prolific of these was Major Allen, who built his own camera and flew his plane over countless farm fields under various lighting conditions in order to create an aerial photographic library of the features, particularly those in the Dorchester area. It is not completely without irony that Major Allen's excursions, a personal hobby that proved to be so vital to our understanding of those long-destroyed features, were funded by the revenue generated by his own corporation, John Allen and Sons, the most exuberant of the gravel extraction companies operating in the area at that time.

The onset of World War II redoubled the nation's need for gravel, and what remained of many Neolithic and Bronze Age features north of Dorchester were stripped away. Aerial photographs (Figure 4) show the rapid destruction of the area adjacent to the Minchin Recreation ground over a period of less than three years. Although the urgency did not lessen after the war, given the massive reconstruction of many areas of Britain, more consideration was given to the proper recording of what was being lost, and from 1946 to 1952 Atkinson observed and recorded, albeit with largely untrained staff, the cluster of Dorchester monuments in advance of their total destruction by quarrying (Atkinson *et al* 1951).

In the decades that followed, excavations around the town were being carried out in advance both of gravel extraction and the construction of the Dorchester bypass (Bradley and Chambers 1988; Whittle *et al* 1992). Both activities were highly destructive to the archaeology of the region, but the recording of the features prior to their destruction was considered sufficient.

Figure 4. Quarrying between 1937 (left), 1943 (centre) and present (right). Note cropmarks in upper left of early photos.(Images courtesy NMR Swindon)

Neolithic Dorchester

The Dorchester area is not unusual in its position as a centre for Neolithic and Bronze Age ritual activity and sites of monumental burial, as sites of this type also existed at Lechlade, Brighthampton, Stanton Harcourt, Cassington, Abingdon, and North Stoke (Benson & Miles 1974). However, of the similar monument sites of the Upper Thames Valley, the Dorchester cursus is the longest (Figure 5). Even without the identification of its northern terminus, at 1605m in length it dwarfs its nearest parallels at nearby Drayton. (Table 1)

Site name	*Completeness*	*Length*	*Width*	*Entrances*
Benson (Crowmarsh)	Complete	1090m	65m	Some
Buscot Wick	Incomplete	650m	50m	Some
Dorchester-on-Thames	Incomplete, northern terminus unidentified	1650m	60m	Multiple
Drayton North	Possibly complete	650m	75m	Multiple
Drayton St Leonard	Incomplete, northern terminus unidentified	410m	45m	Some
Drayton South (Sutton Courtenay)	Possibly complete	750m	70m	Some
Lechlade	Incomplete, southern terminus obscured by development	300m	45m	Multiple
North Stoke	Complete	240m	20m	Some
Stadhampton	complete	385m	40m	One

Table 1. Cursus and related monuments in the Upper Thames Valley (after Barclay et al *2003, 218)*

Dorchester exhibits "the greatest diversity of monuments and the longest sequence of development of all the Upper Thames complexes" (Whittle *et al* 1992, 195) and managed to maintain its significance consistently, by being a place that was likely a major social and economic focus spanning millennia.

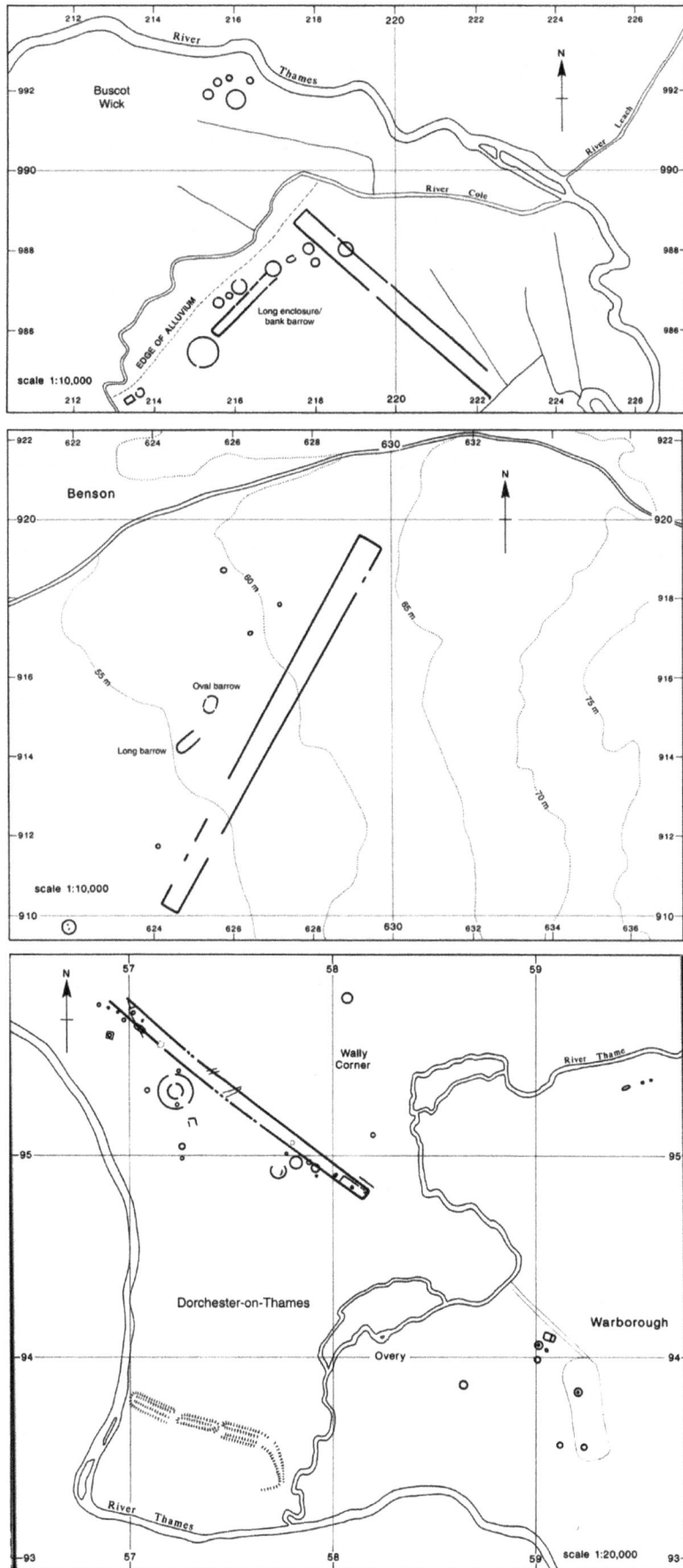

*Figure 5. Plans of some of the cursus monument complexes mentioned in the text
(after Barclay et al 2003, 226-229)*

Loveday suggests that Dorchester may have been a "cult centre" (1999, 55), serving as an inspiration for the other cursus complexes in the region. Set apart from all the others by a 100 degrees of difference in orientation and in its peculiar (convex terminus) form, the Dorchester cursus may have been the progenitor of a series of monuments across the Upper Thames valley. Yet what made Dorchester a prime location for such a significant role? Barclay and Hey (1999) put forth the argument that the siting of the Neolithic monuments within the landscape, at least in the Upper Thames Valley, had much to do with the importance of the river. Certainly the proximity of the Thames and the Thame would have influenced the creators of these features, and the relation between funerary monuments and flowing water is well attested (Parker Pearson *et al* 2006, 229). Alternatively, or perhaps additionally, the proximity and parallel orientation of the two Wittenham Clumps may have factored into the decision, serving as visual manifestations of fertility along the lines of the Paps of Anu in Ireland (Loveday 1999, 59) or less speculatively, as landmarks to guide travellers to the ritual destination.

The pits and burial/cremation circles around the northern fields of Dorchester on Thames have fuelled speculation for a number of years regarding both purpose and dating. Initial investigations by Atkinson (1951) indicated that these pits were postholes of timber circles, possibly burned *in situ* based on the fact that there was no real evidence of posts, and often in reports were referred to as post pipes (Gibson, 1992a, 86). Gibson argues rather convincingly for a primary and secondary usage of these post circles. While at first the holes held posts to form a wood henge of the type seen at Sarn-y-Bryn-Caled (Gibson 1992b), they were subsequently removed and the holes allowed to silt up to some degree, or perhaps even intentionally backfilled. However at a later stage, these holes were re-used to contain cremation burials, a pattern seen in several locations where a proximate relationship existed between a cursus and these round burial sites.

While it is still unclear from the available dating whether the cursus was created piecemeal around the earlier monuments or constructed as a single event (Whittle *et al* 1992, 197 *contra* Loveday 1999, 51), what is certain is the importance to the builders of respecting the earlier features while making their own contribution to the landscape. Case (1986, 27) calculates that based upon the depth of the ditches defining the monuments, the Dorchester cursus could have taken a labour input of 30,000 man-hours. While tempting to see the creation of monuments on such a scale as indicators of a society organised by 'top-down' imposition of power, this need not to have been so. Social differentiation is "as likely to have emerged from the conditions of construction and subsequent use, as to have preceded the decision to build" (Whittle 1996, 276). One might look at an "ethnography" of archaeologists on a non-commercial dig; at the outset, the team begins with notions of egalitarianism, with every member of the project given the freedom to work as they see fit under the over-arching mandate of the research design. Yet it soon becomes apparent that there is little room for egalitarianism if any progress on the dig is to be made, and not long into the project, leaders have emerged and a trench hierarchy has developed. Without this type of organisation, the command structure, there is often a loss of direction and motivation for the 'community' of diggers. Thus it may be that the great monuments in the landscape are not the physical manifestation of a society under the control of 'big men', but rather that these features, with the performative process and organisational challenges that their construction must have produced, may have induced the conditions necessary to encourage the development of the society into more hierarchal groups, a change that was monumental indeed.

Counter to the possibility that the monument was constructed all in one go, with the naissance of group organisation, there is no reason to suppose that Case's estimate relates to a group of 300 people working over the course of a month or a season. It may be rather that the performative element of monument building was stretched over a longer period of time. These monuments may have taken a lifetime, an occurrence not at all alien from medieval cathedral construction, when a man might lay the foundation stones, and his grandchildren would celebrate the completion. Thus the very act of monument creation and perhaps maintenance would re-affirm the community's relationship with the landscape in a participatory performance that might alter in form over the generations, but relayed essentially the same message of belonging. The re-use of space and the attempted continuity of function, perhaps related to the preservation of history in the landscape as well as a mythic element of geographical genealogy (Gosden and Lock 1998), are recurring themes in the Dorchester narrative.

Bronze Age activity

The area to the north of the present village offers evidence of a persistent use of the region for ritual and funerary significance, although it would be extremely careless to imply a direct continuity of use. The Bronze Age ring ditches and their associated barrow burials respect the Neolithic monuments in some cases, but there are ditches, one of which contained a Middle Bronze Age bucket urn (Whittle *et al* 1992, 160), which completely ignore the cursus and indeed cut though it in at least four places (Barclay *et al* 2006,226). A deliberate disregard for the earlier feature may be suggested by this, or possibly, as offered by Loveday (1999, 59) the cursus, was by that time no longer as visually impressive as one might suppose and therefore barely noticed by those who ran a field ditch through it. Since the main axis of the field system apparently shared the same alignment as the nearby henge monument (Bradley and Chambers 1988, 271), than perhaps it is indeed more likely that the ploughing of the cursus was oversight rather than intentional disrespect.

Traditionally, in the Upper Thames Valley region there has been "little sign of pre-Iron age field systems" on the gravels (Robinson 1984, 4). The numerous pre-Roman field systems and ditches noted around Dorchester, and indeed under the settlement itself (Frere 1962, 118-20) have usually been considered to be Iron Age in origin, the ubiquitous 'Celtic field system'. But recently, a study by Bradley and Yates has shown some indications that these field systems may actually date to the Bronze Age, and that these Bronze Age features suggest certain patterns of use based upon their cosmological alignment (2007, 97). They noted a predominance of field systems at major confluences and a general NE-SW alignment in lowland England, along with associated ring works dating to the same period, to metal deposits in nearby rivers and to evidence of fine metalwork, all of which are present in the Dorchester area. Although consideration of this new work may lead to a new interpretation of the Dorchester field systems, one must not be too quick to abandon the Iron Age field system entirely. Collis warns of the "danger of a theoretical totalitarianism being imposed by those who espouse the latest trendy ideas" (2007, 524) and indeed a measure of caution is recommended before casting away the working assumptions of the previous generation.

One must be particularly cautious when interpreting the position in the landscape of features, with relation to the river. The floodplain as we know it now was not present during some parts of the Bronze Age, and thus some locations that are impinged upon by the Thames now may have been dry land, even worked arable land several millennia ago (Bradley 1986, 40), hiding from us the full extent of early agricultural production. Although apparent that a mixture of agrarianism and pastoralism was practiced in the Dorchester area, it has been suggested that for the Early and Middle Bronze Age in this region, a cultural practice of accumulating and maintaining large herds of livestock may have restricted the growth of farming (Robinson 1984, 9). Indeed it is possible that the collapse of a prestige-herd economy, driven by the carrying capacity of territory versus herd size, may have triggered a change in farming practices (Lambrick 1992, 87) as well as channelling the ostentatious display of wealth on the hoof to the possession or deposition of finely crafted metalwork. The abundance of metalwork found in deliberate deposition contexts, particularly in watery places, indicates that this had become a widespread cultural practice in the region by the Late Bronze Age.

A bronze awl recovered in association with a collared urn near the Big Rings site proved, when subjected to metallurgical analysis, to be of considerable interest. Based on the relative proportions of the impurities, particularly those of nickel and antimony, the awl was most likely not of British origin but rather from the continent (Northover 1992, 194). Dating to the Early Bronze Age, that such a simple and mundane implement may have been imported illustrates the fluidity of trade across the channel. A Late Bronze Age bracelet resembling the Odoorn type associated with northern Germanic origin was also discovered at Dorchester (O'Connor 1980, 211), increasing the likelihood that this region had long experienced cross-channel influences.

There has been scant evidence of any Bronze Age settlement on the northern side of the Thames, but the dredging of the riverbed near Days Lock in the nineteenth century yielded a scabbard end and a small buckler or shield boss, indicating some activity in the area during this period (Evans 1881, 343-4). The buckler (Figure 6), complete with handle, is too fragile to have been meant to withstand the rigours of combat on its own and may have adorned a larger wooden or hide shield, although there is little indication of where such an artefact would have been attached. Interestingly, in the nineteenth century , many antiquarians in the region believed that the shield and some contemporary swords and daggers found elsewhere in the Thames were proof positive of the British defence against Aetius Plautus during the Roman conquest. This in turn led to some rather erroneous assumptions about the nature of the earthworks around Dorchester, which shall be further discussed in an upcoming chapter. Thankfully, more careful assessment of such finds has led to our greater understanding of Bronze Age ritual water deposition.

A possibility may be that the fragile buckler was never intended to see combat and was entirely crafted for deposition. Lest one be tempted to forget the harsh realties of Bronze Age combat, however, the Dorchester area has provided us with a vivid, gruesome reminder: at Queenford Farm to the north of the present village, skeletal remains were recovered of an individual pierced through the pelvis with a bronze spear (Manning and Leeds 1921, 240), which was snapped off in the bone, likely during an unsuccessful attempt to retrieve the weapon for further use. Other prolific metal artefacts of this period include celts, or socketed axe-heads (Figure 6), and palstaves of which several are known from the nineteenth century, although admittedly they are provenenced as "in the neighbourhood of" or "near Dorchester, Oxon" (*ibid*, 75-78; 83-86; 109-112). Additionally, a seated burial was found in the Dyke Hills, at a depth of 2.5 metres, without dating evidence but apparently similar to Bronze Age burials from Cassington and Eynsham (Kirk and Leeds 1953, 63). Regrettably, its discovery and excavation under non-archaeological circumstances make it difficult to interpret its significance.

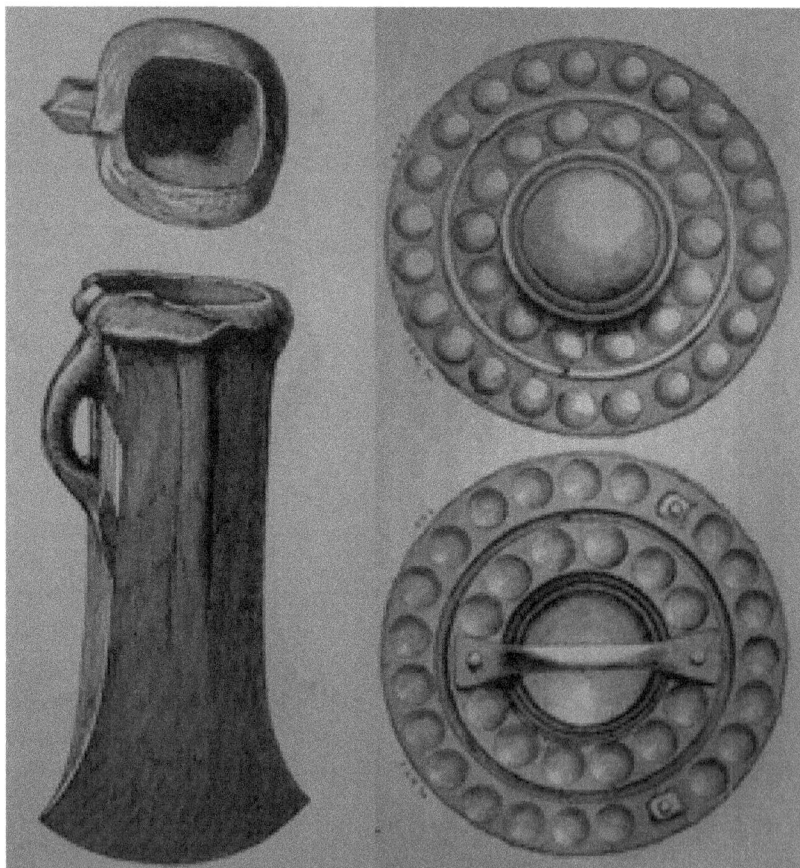

Figure 6. Finds from the Thames at Dorchester (after Evans 1881)

Across the river, the Castle Hill site of the Wittenham Clumps has produced evidence for Late Bronze Age settlement, in the form of a large midden deposit which was spread out over a distance of at least 300 metres (Barclay 2006, 232). Interestingly, this site also produced the earliest Iron Age pottery from the area and its proximity to the Castle Hill Early Iron Age hillfort, as well as clear stratigraphical   relationships suggest a continuity of occupation spanning the Late Bronze Age/ Early

Iron Age transition phase (Hingley 1983, 54). This transition may have been caused by the results of sweeping changes across western Europe, one of which was the 'drying up' of available metal supplies (Bradley 1992, 21). This may have led to a cultural catastrophe, as people were no longer able to express the societal standing through the medium of conspicuous deposition. As the socio-political system collapsed, there was a massive "re-organisation of the landscape in the early iron Age, associated with substantial boundaries" (Hey 2007, 170). Old power bases losing their hold on communities may have spurred "fragmentation and conflict" (*ibid*) leading to amongst other things, the creation of such hillforts as that at Castle Hill. Regardless of the chaos and conflict inherent in the adjustments to the new political and economic systems, it is likely that herdsmen still grazed their livestock, farmers still grew grain and women continued to care for their young ones. Life remained stable, in spite of the instability of its organisation.

Chapter Three

IRON AGE DORCHESTER

"A man may do as he wills with his own; but he should not be allowed so to do with his own as to destroy the right which every man has in the history and monuments of his country."(Saturday Review July 2, 1870, on the destruction of the Dorchester Dykes)

Studies of the Iron Age in the Thames Valley have been extensive, as southern central Britain is seen, often incorrectly, to be the template by which to understand the entire island during that period. The Upper Thames has been well represented both by inclusion in larger syntheses (Cunliffe 2004; 2005; Harding 1974; Champion and Collis 1996) as well as in a series of publications more specific to the region (Harding 1972; Cunliffe and Rowley 1978; Lambrick in press). However, at Dorchester, there has been very little work done on the Iron Age remains, largely due to the inability to access the major settlement enclosed by the Dyke Hills earthworks. Some Iron Age material has been excavated at nearby Mount Farm and at Allen's Pit, so-called for the previously mentioned recorder and destroyer of the Dorchester gravels, but it would seem that the greatest concentration of Iron Age artefacts recovered from Dorchester belong to the later period and consist primarily of coinage.

Allen's Pit does hold the regional distinction of being a rare example of early settlement enclosure. At a time when most settlements were largely open, that at Allen's Pit was fund to have been surrounded by a ditch 3m deep and 5m wide. Even compared to the dimensions of middle Iron Age ditches, when enclosed settlements became more common, the Allen's Pit enclosure is exceptional. Perhaps it was the proximity to landmarks and monuments traditionally utilised by the wider population that made the founders of this settlement feel the need to elaborately demarcate what belonged to them.

Figure 7. Iron Age earthworks at Castle Hill in foreground and, the Dyke Hills earthworks in background with the village of Dorchester beyond. (Courtesy Ian Cartwright)

As mentioned above, Castle Hill (Figure 7) across the Thames presented some of the earliest Iron Age ceramics, which appear to pre-date some of the Early Iron Age pottery found at Allen's Pit (Bradford 1942, 38-9) although this site produced sherds across the "whole Iron Age series in this area" (Leeds 1935, 41). One may suppose that the Allen's Pit site indicates a continuity of occupation throughout the entire span of the Iron Age, but although possible, it is unwise to place too much weight on a single site now lost due to quarrying. Further excavation in the area may be able to confirm longevity of settlement, but for now caution should be exercised.

There is a growing body of scholars who support the suggestion that the earlier Iron Age was a time of relative egalitarianism and peace with a communal social structure; large enclosed tracts of land suggest communal farming (Bradley and Yates 2007, 100) and a paucity of weaponry as compared to the Late Bronze Age and Late Iron Age (Hill 1995, 49) hint at a peaceful lifestyle. This view rejects the notion of a societal hierarchy and sees the hillforts as places of social congregation rather than refuges from attack or venues of territorial dominance. Against this concept of the peaceful Iron Age are scholars who believe it is counter to everything we know about human behaviour either past or present to suggest a total absence of violence and warfare (Sharples 1991, 79-80; James 2007, 171). While there may be no evidence to support the idea of a powerful chieftain sitting as lord of the domain atop Castle Hill, it may be an overly simplistic rejection of past theory to deny the likelihood of a violent and tumultuous Dorchester during the earlier Iron Age. As this was a time of great demarcation of the land, whether with the intent to farm communally or not, there was likely tension between other large groups, and the farmers may have retreated across the river to the hillfort as necessary. Clearly, at some point the inhabitants of the area decided to erect an earthen defence on the north side of the river. Whether this was accomplished in the Middle or Late Iron Age is, at present, unknown due to a lack of investigation, but the significance of their construction cannot be doubted.

Dyke Hills

With inner banks rising over 3 metres from the level ground, and an outer bank nearly a metre higher, the double-ramparted earthworks known as Dyke Hills dominate the landscape on the northern shore of the Thames, mirroring the imposing Early Iron Age hillfort across the river on the Wittenham Clumps. A broad ditch runs between the two banks and at least one causeway connects them. An external ditch runs along the outer bank to the north. There appears to have been "cross banks" at the eastern end of the earthworks, suggesting an entrance point (Sutton 1966, 31) against the Thame; the gaps visible today are products of relatively modern destruction. There have been no properly conducted excavations of these earthen dykes that would permit an accurate dating of the features. Indeed for a very long time scholars of the eighteenth and nineteenth century believed them to be part of a Roman camp. When local historian and Secretary of the Oxford Architectural and Historic Society, Mr Barnes, suggested in a letter to historian J H Parker that he believed the Dyke hills to be of British origin and of similar purpose as the hillfort defences on Castle Hill across the river, he was summarily dismissed. Parker wrote that while Barnes' views "deserved consideration", more learned men with "very high authority on the subject" did not agree and thus the site was most definitely a Roman camp built for the conquest (Parker 1882, xxiv). Mr Barns is vindicated in that we now believe his assessment to be the correct one, yet how frustrating that over a century on, we still have no real dating!

The earthworks enclose a space over 114 acres in area and appears to contain an abundance of features of uncertain date. A series of aerial photographs from the 1920s and 30s were the first to reveal the complexity and density of the features (Figure 8), while a more recent group of photographs taken during a particularly dry July in 2003 has shown in even more detail the staggering number of pits, ditches, and probable round houses. This heavy concentration of features within an enclosed area has led to the now-fossilised assumption that Dyke Hills was an urban, or at least a 'proto-urban' centre or *oppidum*. While there is no compelling evidence to reject this interpretation out of hand, its present status as absolute fact is completely with out foundation, as there is no evidence to confirm the urban nature of this settlement.

Figure 8. Dyke Hills from the NW (above) – note the damage to the western portion . cropmarks from 1936 (left) and 2003. (courtesy NMR Swindon)

The possibility exists, as we have no excavation or survey data to suggest otherwise, that the profligate nature of the cropmarks visible within the '*oppidum*' are indicative of a series of features existent over a long period of time, rather than a wealth of urban activity contemporaneously occurring within the enclosed space. Similar evidence has been seen elsewhere, such as at Thornhill Farm, where, simply based on the aerial photography, one might have assumed an area of dense population, but excavation revealed a small "wandering settlement", in use over a long period of time (Jennings *et al* 2004). What, then, might this imply about the status of the Dyke Hills *oppidum*? It has been suggested that there may be earlier Iron Age origins of the Dyke Hills settlements, as at nearby Abingdon (Lambrick *et al* in prep). Only excavation will reveal the dating sequence and significance of the buildings and pits observed from the air. Indeed, at present we do not even know the extent of the settlement as it approaches the Thames banks, for without a better understanding of the river levels during the Iron Age, it is unclear how much of the land adjacent to the river was submerged or unusable.

For nearly a century and a half, the Dyke Hills and its settlement have remained untouched by archaeological investigation. This due not to a lack of desire on the part of academics, but rather a refusal of permission by two generations of landowners whose recalcitrance spans at least 50 years. In 1958, the landowner requested permission from the Ministry of Works to build a small cottage within the Dyke Hills enclosure. Although a careful strategy could have been implemented that would have accommodated both the farmer's need for a cottage and the desire of academics to excavate, the Ministry instead sent a rather terse letter of denial. This began a cold war between the landowner's family and archaeology that has at times escalated to the point of implied violence and continues to the present generation. One would hope that this incompatibility between agrarian and academic interests need not continue in perpetuity, but that an olive branch might be extended and received to the betterment of all. Hawkes, of the Institute of Archaeology at Oxford, particularly hoped to begin a campaign of excavations in the late 1950s but was met with staunch refusal, perhaps because of his accusations that the landowner was deliberately trying to ruin the landmark. A letter from Hawkes to the Keeper of the

Ashmolean Museum references the (perceived) intentional driving of cattle onto the dykes by the landowner, for the sole purpose of destroying the dykes. Whether the intent was in fact malicious or not, a request from the Ministry of Works prompted the removal of the herd. A visit to the site today makes clear that, if the earthworks have remained untouched by archaeologists, they have not fared so from nature. Animal incursions, both from the above-mentioned livestock and from the most intensive rabbit settlement since Watership Down, have done extensive damage to the integrity of the earthworks and have exacerbated erosion. Yet this is nothing, compared with the destruction that began in 1870 when the landowner at that time, Mr Latham, began the process of rendering the Dykes into arable topsoil (Figure 9).

Figure 9. Labourers reducing the earthworks at Dyke Hills – 1871 (courtesy Ashmolean Museum)

When the levelling of the Dykes came to the attention of the antiquarians of Oxford, much outrage was voiced, particularly in editorial columns of the newspapers of the day. In 1870, General Pitt-Rivers, renowned antiquarian and often hailed as the "Father of British Archaeology", went to see the devastation for himself, and after recording a section of what had been exposed, sent a letter to Latham, highlighting the significance of the site and appealing for a cessation of demolition. The plea apparently fell on deaf ears, and in 1871, a memo to the Home Secretary from the Society of Antiquaries in London called for the government to take a more pro-active role in the protection of ancient places of national importance: "We venture to suggest to Her Majesty's Ministers the desirability of a Royal Commission being appointed, for the purpose of ascertaining the present condition of those important Monuments of Antiquity, which, if destroyed, could not be replaced, and also the effectual means of preserving them from further decay and injury" (Pantin 1939, 13). The result, ultimately, was the creation of what we now know as English Heritage and the scheduling of ancient monuments. Latham was left with no alternative, and the destruction of the Dyke Hills ended. Lest one come away with a villainous image of Mr Latham, one must recall that in the nineteenth century, the importance of heritage management was never made clear to those outside the intelligentsia. Latham likely did not hate the past, he simply wanted more use of his arable land. Indeed, the family were such good farmers that Latham's father is quoted with great admiration in

Young's famous agricultural works on the region (Young 1813). With such a reputation to live up to, it is little wonder that Latham simply wanted to expand upon the family's agricultural standing. Yet met with such resistance and hostility from the antiquarians, the farmer became entrenched in his position. This is truly a lesson of how modern archaeology can improve on the techniques of the past as we strive to include landowners and farmers in understanding their role as caretakers of the nation's heritage.

Figure 10. The Dyke Hills at Dorchester after their partial destruction in 1870-1.
(Photograph by Henry William Taunt, courtesy Oxfordshire County Council Photographic Archive)

The Victorian photographer Henry Taunt captured the neglected hulk of the desecrated monument in his collection of Thames Valley images as short time after work had ceased (Figure 10); the damage was, of course, irreparable but some knowledge was gained from this action founded in ignorance. Latham's labourers, though instructed to keep anything of interest, obviously were uninterested in a great deal, as they reported that they found nothing, yet when on a few occasions their labours were observed by the anxious antiquarians from Oxford, a great many things were recovered. This suggests that, to use Hearne's phrase concerning Dorchester field labourers a century earlier, they were "altogether ignorant of the use of such remains of Antiquity [taking] no manner of care to preserve them but broke them to pieces before anyone of Skill and Curiosity could have a view of them" (Hearne 1711, 163). Unfortunately, many of the skilful and curious antiquarians of the day had far fewer qualms about the respectful treatment of human remains. Occasionally, interested observers would retrieve a skull or entire skeleton from the workmen's barrows and add it to their private collections, with no further exploration of its context or association with other items. There are in the Oxfordshire County Museum, two human *crania* [2] with a spidery ink script on the bone reading "Dike [sic] Hills June 1871". Additionally, several more skeletons went to Rolleston of the Oxford Natural Museum and some were taken by William Garnet, an undergraduate student who was curious about the bones and enthusiastic about their discovery, but perhaps not quite as respectful in their curation as one could hope. In 1921, E T Leeds, in an attempt to track down these skeletons, contacted Garnett, but was disappointed to discover that the skeletons had been lost after their use in an undergraduate prank. Mr Garnett recalled "assembling one skeleton and placing it in the house of a tutor, causing great amusement and no little consternation to the occupant of the rooms". (Dorchester Archive,

---

[2] These were given to the Museum as part of an extensive lot of varied artefacts by F. Underhill, an antiquarian of the Warwickshire region, but it is uncertain how they came to be in his possession. There is one nearly whole skull, that seemed to this writer to be male and another partial skull, possibly female, badly repaired with globs of yellowing glue along the upper palette.

Ashmolean Museum) Clearly, not the best practice for the curation of human remains! Of the bones whose locations are known, none have been put to rigorous scientific dating analysis, and thus the only dating for them relies upon the associated materials, clearly apparent in only two instances, which were Late Roman/ Early Medieval and will be discussed in a later chapter.

Other known artefacts from the Dyke Hills demolition include some pot sherds that Pitt- Rivers (then Lane Fox) felt certain were of "undoubtedly British origin" (Lane Fox 1870, 415) and an abundance of flint scatter from the manufacture of implements. What other items of interest the labourers may have recovered no doubt were either thrown into the river, where some pieces of iron and skeletons were said to have been discarded, or pocketed and either kept as curiosities or sold off to collectors with no record of their provenance. An 1874 letter to Rolleston of the Oxford University Museum from MacFarlane, the Abbey vicar, acknowledges that, "not long ago a 'Boadicea' [sic] gold coin was found" at the Dykes and sold to an Oxford dealer for £25, a considerable price for the times. Such behaviour was not uncommon even in the days before metal detectors. There were reports of Iron Age gold coins recovered from the banks as well and the ploughing of the interior for agriculture has yielded a prodigious amount if Iron Age coinage, among the most dense distributions in Britain (Cook and Rowley 1985, 16). Bronze coinage can be taken as an indication of a budding moneyed economy (Collis 1971, 79), and at Dorchester there have been finds of at least a dozen such coins[3] (Manning and Leeds 1921, 240; Miles 1986, 45) indeed, this author has seen in a private amateur collection a number of Iron Age coins purportedly recovered from various locations around the village of Dorchester during building and gardening activities over the past twenty-five years. However, the holder of these items permitted only a brief and cursory inspection and has since refused access to the materials for reasons one can only guess at. These coins do hint at a greater presence of coinage in this region during the Iron Age than previously suspected, but without a more detailed inspection, one can only speculate as to what this means for the overall interpretation of coin use at the Dyke Hills. More than a simple mechanism for regulating trade, coins are powerful items of expression for social and cultural identity, marking a shift away from a pattern of regional identities and local biographies, to "power relationships based primarily on individuals" (Moore 2007, 55).

Continental connections and trade

Harding referred to a different "district around Dorchester on Thames, where new cultural influences from the south-east were more readily absorbed or imposed" (1974, 28). What was the nature of these influences, how were they brought to Dorchester, and what made the region so much more open to external influence than neighbouring areas? One might be tempted to see the Dorchester area as one where new influences and artefacts had been coming for a long time; positioned as it is along the Thames waterway, the communities that sprang up here over the centuries were accustomed to interaction with other groups, both from the "cultural backwaters" further upriver as well as the more cosmopolitan influences coming up from ultimately continental sources.

A column in the Times written by Arthur Evans, observed that there was perhaps a larger extent of Greek and Italian influences upon pre-Roman Britain than was being realised. As part of his evidence he offered the Dorchester find of a "fine black glazed ware with a foliated white ornament round its inner margin" (Evans 1893). He believed it to date to 200BC and felt that the context in which it was recovered was secure enough to rule out completely accidental loss of a "Grand Tour" souvenir. This was not the only find to suggest Middle to Late Iron Age trade in continental objects, as a Greek cup and an Italic cup have also been dredged from the Thames (Bradley and Smith 2007, 32). Previously rejected as recent discards, current thinking is more open to the likelihood of a much longer pattern of exchange across the Channel. Despite Hill's (2007, 17) doubts as to the existence of Iron Age elites, or to their desire to possess (or be *seen* to possess- an important difference when contemplating concepts of identity) exotic goods, there is a compelling amount of artefactual evidence to suggest a lively trade in such items, a trade that likely was driven by a demand. However a desire for these types of goods at one location was not necessarily indicative of a wholesale "Continentalisation" of the region, as it

---

[3] A newspaper clipping from 1871,credited to the pseudonym "Colossus", mentions "a small urn containing coins was found" during the destruction of the Dykes which he presumed "the Goth of a farmer himself has kept" (Dorchester Archive, Ashmolean Museum).

appears that choices made by individual communities varied widely across relatively small geographic areas. The abundance of continental fine wares adopted at Dorchester in the very late pre-Roman conquest phase seem to be in stark contrast to the paucity of similar items at such nearby sites as Gravelly Guy (Lambrick and Allen 2004, 333). Access to the goods of the wider world likely helped some individuals increase their prestige, contributing to the eventual abandonment of the egalitarian model, as the one-upmanship of exploiting and attracting connections, as well as accumulating and selectively distributing exotic items, the physical manifestation of those connections, fuelled a hierarchal society, with the more prestigious men attracting the most followers.

Contrary to evidence of a thriving river-borne trade in exotica, Booth advances an argument that the Thames River would not have been a major travel and transport route based upon its general poor navigability. He cites the unimportance of the river in linking Roman station and cities, implying that if the river were an easy route, the Romans would have used it more (P Booth, *pers com.*) Indeed, this argument carries some weight, particularly if one considers just how much construction and engineering had to go into various lock systems in order to make the Thames navigable today. Admittedly, the course, depth and speed of the Thames has undoubtedly changed in the past 2200 years, but without good riverside evidence[4] of functioning waterborne transportation, Booth's suggestion is rather compelling, and begs a reconsideration of the conventional interpretation of the Dyke Hills enclosure as being set up to regulate the route node for river trade at the confluence of the Thames and the Thame.

Evans also noted that among the prodigious amounts of coin found at Dorchester, there were specimens of "ancient British tin money with designs imitated from the coinage of Massalia" (Evans 1893). They hint at an element of the population who by the end of the Middle or the beginning of the Late Iron Age had access to fine quality continental wares and was aware of external stylistic, lifestyle, and economic diversity. Was Dorchester on Thames a cultural hotspot, the last stop before the virtual backwaters of Abingdon and beyond? Yet Abingdon too enjoyed a similar position in the Iron Age landscape of the Thames Valley. Similarly placed at the confluence of the Ock and the Thames, a defended settlement has been identified that has striking similarities to the Dyke Hills. Inner and outer ditches form a defensive bow strung by the Thames (Figure 11). A defensive bank seems to have been pushed into the ditches to level them sometime in the second century AD (Allen 2000, 24), indicating that space was needed for settlement expansion. This raises the curious difference between Abingdon and Dorchester: why did the enclosed settlement at Abingdon continue to develop into the period of Roman influence, whereas at Dorchester, occupation appears to cease within the Dyke Hills and is relocated to the north, at the site of the village today?

---

[4] An 1894 handwritten note from a Mr Hewett suggests that "about 150 yards south of the point where the boundary between Long and Little Wittenham cuts the river Thames" a number of piles were found in the riverbed. Yet there is no further information and with out any way to date the alleged piling, one cannot reliable offer this observance as evidence of a pre-historic water landing (Dorchester Archive, Ashmolean Museum).

CASSINGTON:The Big Enclosure

DORCHESTER:Dyke Hills

ABINGDON

Defensive ditches

— certain
— conjectured

0 ———————— 1000m

SALMONSBURY

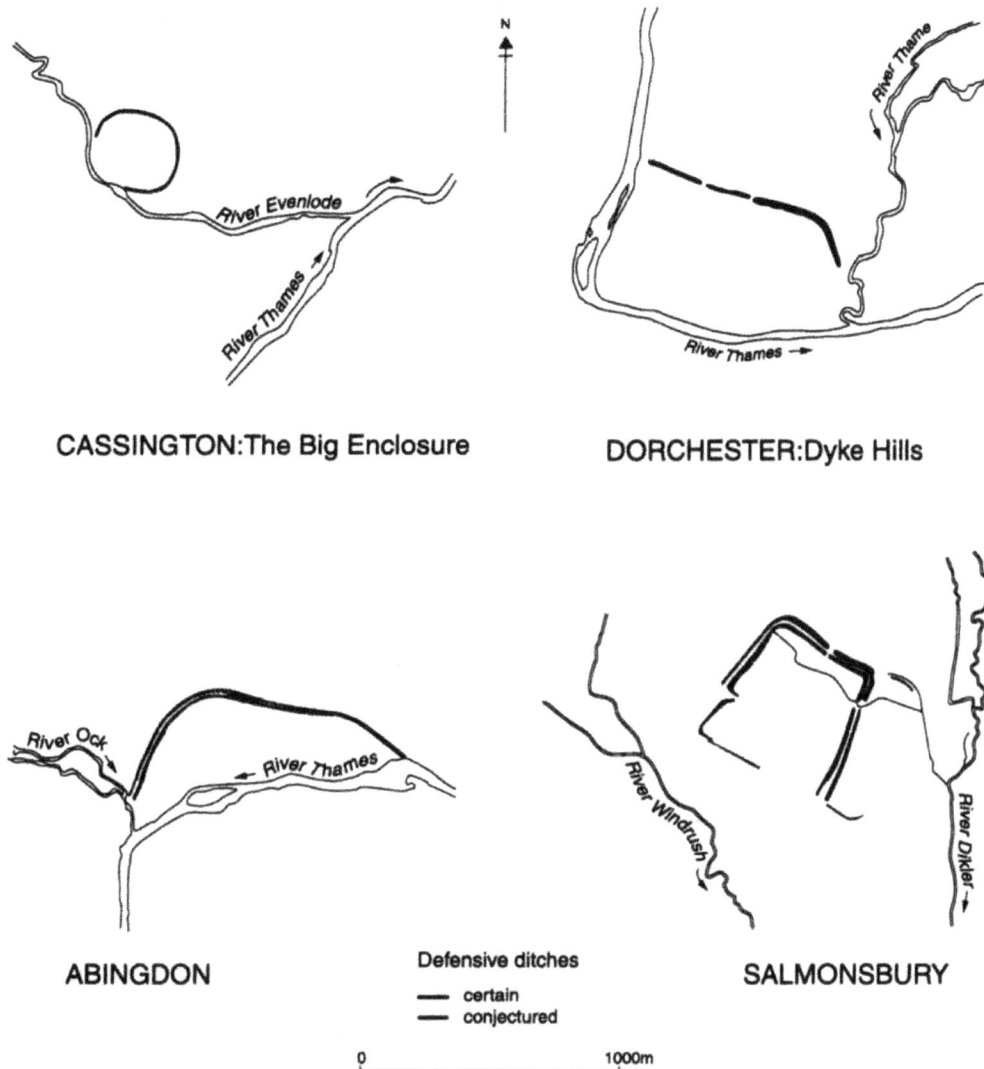

*Figure 11. Plans of Dyke Hills and similar late Iron Age defended settlements in the region.
(after Allen 2000, 25)*

Tribal boundaries

Dorchester is believed to have owed much of its fame and significance during the Iron Age to the fact that it marked the boundary of two if not three tribal territories. Here at the confluence of the Thames and Thame, we are told, the lands of the Atrebates, the Catevellauni and the Dobunni met. This alone could have afforded Dorchester the respect and awe due such liminal places, not only a political liminality, but a natural one as well. Indeed, Dorchester could be described as a critical route node, marking a intersection of natural waterways, man-made trackways and a dominant natural landmark in the form of the Wittenham Clumps. While there is no reason to doubt the role of the rivers in creating a spiritual *gravitas* to the location, the role of tribal borders must be examined. It could be argued that one of the self-imposed limits that have greatly hindered a better understanding of later Iron Age societies in the Thames Valley, indeed in most of Britain, is the incursion of the historical literature upon this pre-historic culture. By embracing the tribal names and tentative borders offered by the Classical historians and observers, we force ourselves to view Iron Age Britain consistently through the eyes of an outsider. It is time to let the material culture speak for the identity of the indigenous people; perhaps, the tribal maps need to be eliminated from our picture of southern Britain, at least in the relatively static form they currently hold. It may be that the Roman idea of the tribal unit, and why they had so many difficulties with tribal factionalism in the honouring of agreements made with leaders, is that the Roman concept of what constituted a tribe and defined a leader was culturally

23

different from what defined these things for a native Briton. An analogy might be drawn from the Native tribes of North America, where in many cases treaties were reached between white authorities and (they presumed) a tribal entity, only to discover that the arrangement was really only with that individual and his supporters, as no one man or group had the authority to speak for all in such weighty matters as land accession and tributes. The tribe was then seen to have reneged on a deal that in fact had never been binding and thus naturally, hostilities ensued. It is possible that there were affiliations between small groups in Britain that were, in the Roman quest for organisation, lumped together into tribal entities that had little real meaning for the people who purportedly belonged to them.

The explanation for why "many communities apparently accepted or rejected broader cultural practices at much the same time" (Moore 2007, 41) may lie in the consideration that in spite of apparent tribal division indicated by Classical texts and coin distributions, there may have been distinct differences in communities, even where those communities shared a similar affiliation to a power base, likely in the form of an individual. The evidence exists to indicate that real power in Late Iron Age Britain, at least in the south and east, was determined not so much by territorial location but by personalities. Diodorus Siculus wrote that the power in Britain was held by "many kings and potentates" who for the most part live peacefully among themselves (Creighton 2006, 27). The individual supremacy of a chief or king might have blurred simple concepts of 'tribal' affiliation and set loyalties to lines of descent rather than to tribal territories (Collis 2007, 526)

The argument put forth rather creatively by Henig (2002) and advanced brilliantly by Creighton (2006) is that of the inculcation of *Romanitas* in these powerful personalities, even before the conquest of AD 43. Prior to Caesar's ostentatious exploratory campaigns, the political infrastructure of the area was likely based upon regional petty kings and men of influence, whose control of surpluses gave them power over their followers. Creighton suggests that although Caesar's so-called victory of the Britons had little real impact on daily goings-on, the belief in Rome that Britain was a new possession required the placement of Roman-friendly regional rulers (2006, 23-4), who would serve a "king of kings" and administrate for Rome. Henig illustrates how these implanted rulers created dynasties, whose heirs were sent to Rome in their youth, to be raised with the societal values, cultural tastes and, most importantly for the budding Empire, a certain degree of loyalty to Rome. Over time, the decision of where the power in Britain resided shifted from one made in Britain and approved by Rome, to one simply made in Rome. This had the effect of sowing dissension among the powerful households of southern and central Britain, and when Verica, citing civil unrest, appealed to the Roman Emperor for aid in sorting out the disagreements, Claudius was handed the pretext he needed in order to prove his military prowess and incorporate Britain more permanently and inescapably into its western possessions.

Naturally, some groups would have resented both Verica's choice in running to Rome for foreign help, and the presence of Roman troops in large numbers upon their territories, but some locations, already used to dealing with Romans for perhaps as long as half a century, would have seen no major threat in the addition of some Roman order to the chaos at the top. In the first century BC, at the *oppidum* Magdalensburg in Noricum (present day Austria), a trading post with Rome had grown into a small Roman settlement outside what could be described as a manufacturing town (Alföldy 1966). Over the years, Roman traders took up residence; as they accumulated wealth, they began to want the comforts of home, bringing in their craftsmen and their slaves, until a 'Little Rome' grew up at Magdalensberg. These inhabitants began to take a more active role in the settlement's organisation over time, and when Augustus decided to annex Noricum into the Empire, there was little resistance to the idea. Those living at the heart of Noricum had become comfortable with Roman ways and as Rome let them keep their own (largely impotent) rulers, there would be little need for exchange of hostilities.

Similarly, it has been suggested that Silchester too could have fit this pattern, since much evidence has been found for pre-Claudian continental goods (Fulford 1993, 19) and even the presence of Roman military, perhaps as guards for traders, or as the personal protection of a friendly potentate (Creighton 2006, 67-8). Strabo wrote that there was so much revenue to be made from the heavy duties placed on the exports to, and the imports from, Gaul, including amber, glassware, and "other such trinkets" that there was no need to garrison the island and that Rome would have lost money if they had tried to collect tribute (Ireland 1986, 37). It may not be implausible that the inhabitants of Dorchester, which was already a nexus for trade, faced the Roman advancement with a similar reaction as the people of Magdalensberg and Silchester. By the time they felt their independence slipping away, it was already gone.

Chapter Four

ROMAN DORCHESTER

"The rays of the midday sun fell brightly upon the fair city of Durocina, situated at the junction of the streams which formed the Tameisis; they fell upon its theatre, its basilica, its temples its walls and fortifications...[and] upon the hard stone pavement of the Forum" (Crake 1874, 78-9)

Antiquarian observations

Documents suggest that as early as the sixteenth century, some members of the intellectual communities of Britain had more than a passing interest in the relics of her ancient past. During the reign of Elizabeth I, a petition was made requesting the creation of an academy for the study of antiquities. Keen not to impinge upon the preserve of the academic community, the document was couched in terms designed not to ruffle the feathers of those establishments of higher education that were concerned with nobler disciplines; the petition sought to establish a society that was not intended to be "hurtful to either of the universities [Oxford and Cambridge]...for this society tendeth to the preservance of history and antiquity, of which the universities take little care or regard" (Hearne 1775, 326).

Even earlier, in 1533, Henry VIII appointed John Leland to the unique post of "Royal Antiquary". Travelling to the furthest reaches of Britain, Leland not only created a fascinating itinerary of the places he visited, but also catalogued the vast quantity of antiquities, primarily in the possession of the churches and monasteries, many of which were likely destroyed in the subsequent Dissolution. Although occasionally these observations are no more than snippets of information, they are so precious because Leland was eyewitness to a Britain free from the metal detector, the modern developer, and the gravel extractor, as well as experiencing 450 fewer years of erosion.

Leland's observances of Dorchester provide perhaps the very first documented acknowledgement of the town's prodigious amounts of buried antiquities. As the Roman name of Dorchester was, and indeed still remains, unknown, and having only Bede's Dorcic to go on, Leland bestowed the name *Hydropolis*, his own take on the suggestion that the *Dor* element of the name stemmed from a native word for water[5] (Gelling 1953, 152). Regardless of the spurious appellation, Leland did make mention of the proclivity of the field south of the town for giving up "*numismata Romanorurm* of gold, silver and brasse [sic]" (Hearne 1711, 64).

William Camden, in an attempt to ensure that English gentlemen were not "strangers in their own country" (McCarthy *et al* 2007, 15) set out to document the physical remains of England's ancient past. Camden's observations of antiquities on his travels throughout Britain were documented in a county-by-county catalogue. In this "chorographical description" of Britain in 1586, he noted that the decline of Dorchester was so dramatic from "being anciently a city, it hardly keeps the name of town, though it has proofs enough of its ancient extent in the ruins in the adjoining fields" (Gough 1806, 9). Although Haverfield referred to Camden as one whose "ingenuity has enriched the history of Roman

---

[5] It has been suggested that rather than *Dor* for water, Dorcic may have its origin in the root *derk-* found in Welsh *drych*, and may give Dorcic the interpretation "bright" or "splendid place" (Ekwall 1936)

Britain with numerous errors" (Haverfield 1895, 221), Camden's lists and sketches of Roman coins found in the area were to fuel the interest of generations of antiquarians to come, as *Britannia* became the primary text for those whose interests were so engaged. A companion text, *Britannia Romana* was published in 1732 by John Horsley, containing scores of sketches of inscriptions, coins and other artefacts found all over the country. Horsley's book contained the first published example of an inscription from Oxfordshire, the Dorchester altar, which is discussed in further detail below.

Another major contributor to the archaeological history of Dorchester was Thomas Hearne, an Oxfordshire antiquarian who, as a non-juror, had turned down both the librarianship at the Bodleian and the Camden professorship of ancient history. He instead turned his perceptive intelligence to the editing and compiling of some of the major historical works of previous centuries and it his he whom we have to thanks for the clarity of Leland's *Itineraries*. At the end of his volumes he often inserted additional information he had personally gathered on the antiquities of the region. He also kept copious and thorough diaries, in which he often mentions walks he took to Dorchester to meet a Mr Bannister, an elderly gentleman who always had some item of antiquity to show him. Often, Hearne would take these items back with him to add to his collection. Hearne wrote of witnessing the discovery of many coins at Dorchester, which he remarked were "generally founds on the Southwest part of the town in a field of a black soil, in which is likewise a variety of other remains of antiquity" (Hearne 1711, 163). An avid numismatist, Hearne also used his frequent walks to create a view of the ancient landscape. This seemingly modern concept was to help Hearne reach some unlikely and wholly incorrect conclusions, such as his belief that based on fragmentary stone ruins around the Dorchester area, the walls of the town must have enclosed an area from Overy to Berinsfield. Yet despite such errors, Hearne was one of the first observers to note the link between variation in crop growth and the presence of ancient remains beneath the soil (Salter 1907, 354).

In 1747, a new document came to light which appeared to answer the question about the Roman name for Dorchester. Predating even Leland was the fourteenth century historical writer Richard of Cirencester, whose manuscript *De situ Britanniae (The Description of Britain)* gave an itinerary of travel across Britain and listed "Durocina" for Dorchester on Thames (Bertram 1809, 164). However, in 1866, the document was exposed as a forgery written in 1747 by Charles Bertram, an English teacher living in Denmark. Sadly, Bertram's forgery has overshadowed the work of the real Richard of Cirencester, whose manuscript *Speculum Historiale de Gestis Regum Angliae (A History of the deeds of the English Kings) originally* published between 1355 and 1400, was a genuine if relatively insignificant history of the English. Endorsed as it was by the renowned authority on antiquities at the time, Dr William Stukely, generations of historians and antiquarians, including Edward Gibbon, were misled by this forgery. In spite of it's debunking in 1866, as late as 1872 the manuscript was still being published (Giles), leading many to accept without question the name of Durocina.

The myth of glorious Durocina persisted both in the imaginations of antiquarians and the inhabitants of the nineteenth century village; even to the present day, the word "Durocina", though obscured by many layers of paint, can been seen marked on the lintel over the main door at 33 High Street, Dorchester. The fantasy also thrived on the pages of the popular fiction of the day. Dorchester enthusiast and vicar of nearby Cholsey, AD Crake was the author of several novels of the genre known as Christian historical fiction and focussed on different periods of Dorchester's history. His fanciful novels, filled with brave British youths and wide-eyed slave girls, also recounted the past glories of the Roman town, including a description of the forum, temple, and baths. Crake's musings were credited in his prefaces as having been based in such facts as were supplied to him by fellow vicar and avid collector of antiquities, Rev W C Macfarlane, of Dorchester Abbey.

A more scientific approach

Macfarlane was a member of the Oxford Architecture and Archaeological Society and in 1881 published a pamphlet about the Abbey and its environs, which included some of his observances about the Roman town. This was followed the next year by a more complete history of Dorchester, which included a letter from Mr Barns, a resident of Dorchester who suggested that he could demonstrate that the defences of a legionary camp were preserved in the streets and banks around the village

(Parker 1882, 39). The 1921 edition of *Archaeologia*, in a survey of Oxfordshire archaeology, reported, "no Roman town or buildings of prime importance occur within the county" (Manning and Leeds 1921, 230), but Hogg and Stevens were able to confirm that the town was indeed Roman, defended, and important. This was accomplished by the re-discovery of Barns's claim nearly a half-century later by the Oxford University Archaeological Society, prompting a 1935 campaign of survey and excavation which confirmed the existence of the Roman defences, although refuting most of Barns' "pardonable but erroneous" assumptions (Hogg and Stevens 1937, 41) about the size and characteristics of the Roman ditches. The results of this excavation were not without their own pardonable errors, for while the ramparts were initially dated to AD 125 (*ibid*, 72), Frere later dated them AD 185, largely on the basis of three sherds of black burnished ware (1964, 130). While this date tied in nicely with some historical accounts of violent upheaval in Britain, a later re-examination of the pottery placed the construction date a bit earlier to around AD 150-160 (Hartley 1983, 89).

Thwarted by previously mentioned difficulties in excavating within the Dyke Hills earthworks, C F C Hawkes, himself a resident of Dorchester (number 12, the Priory) turned his attention to the other mysteries of the town. When in 1958, sewer drains were placed under High street, practically outside his front door, a watching brief was undertaken and the line of the walled eastern defences may have been indicated by what he observed. These drainage improvements to the town began to raise fears about the speed with which development might soon follow, particularly on the area of town that belonged to the allotments, and which, in addition to most likely being Hearne's south-western field of black earth, had been undeveloped at least as far back as the earliest tithe maps indicated. Prior to the feared development, Hawkes formed an excavation committee that set about raising funds for an archaeological investigation of the area and appointed Sheppard Frere to carry out fieldwork in the uncultivated areas of the village allotments during 1962-3 (Frere, *pers comm*).

At the same time the Oxford University Archaeological Society was conducting an excavation at the Abbey to discover more about the monastic building there (Cunningham and Banks 1972). They revealed important Roman features and material, but as the thrust of their interest lay with the later phases of the site, the Roman material was handed over to Frere for incorporation into his next Dorchester publication. Sadly, nearly 20 years passed before the second publication, and whilst the pottery assemblage from the Abbey well was detailed (Frere 1984, 127-9), the rather interesting small finds, which apparently included a red cloisonné fine bow brooch from the Rhineland, never got a mention. Frere himself has expressed some reservations about the 1984 publication, which according to him was largely put together by other parties (*pers comm*). One wonders what a proper discussion of the other finds might have added to the story of the eastern edge of Dorchester.

Frere's work was, and remains, the most significant programme of excavations within Roman Dorchester to date. Much of the evidence upon which the following sections will be based originates with Frere's findings, but it would be irresponsible to accept all his interpretations nearly fifty years on without realising the potential fossilisation of facts and without exploring the possibility that some of the interpretations might be open to question.

After Frere's work in the Roman town, it was nearly a decade before the next major excavation within the village. In the early 1970's, the efforts of a few dedicated archaeologists had resulted in the formation of a "rescue archaeology unit", out of which grew a commercial unit, currently called Oxford Archaeology. Prior to major developments in Dorchester, archaeological evaluations took place under the auspices of this unit and in 1972 there were two simultaneous projects underway, offering the potential to answer many of the questions lingering about Dorchester. One was in the northwest of the town, inside the ramparts while the other was in the south, where the line of defence turned north to form the eastern rampart. Neither excavation was without tribulation; regrettably, both resulted in inconclusive interpretations.

In the last decade of the twentieth century and the beginning of the twenty-first, small scale watching briefs continued to document the state of development in Dorchester. Many of these evaluations amounted to little more than a test pit, a drainage line or the footprint of a building. In some cases, the work was carried out extremely well, but in others, poor strategies, doubtlessly driven by inexperienced staff and budgetary concerns, led to a failure to maximise the opportunities afforded by development.[6]

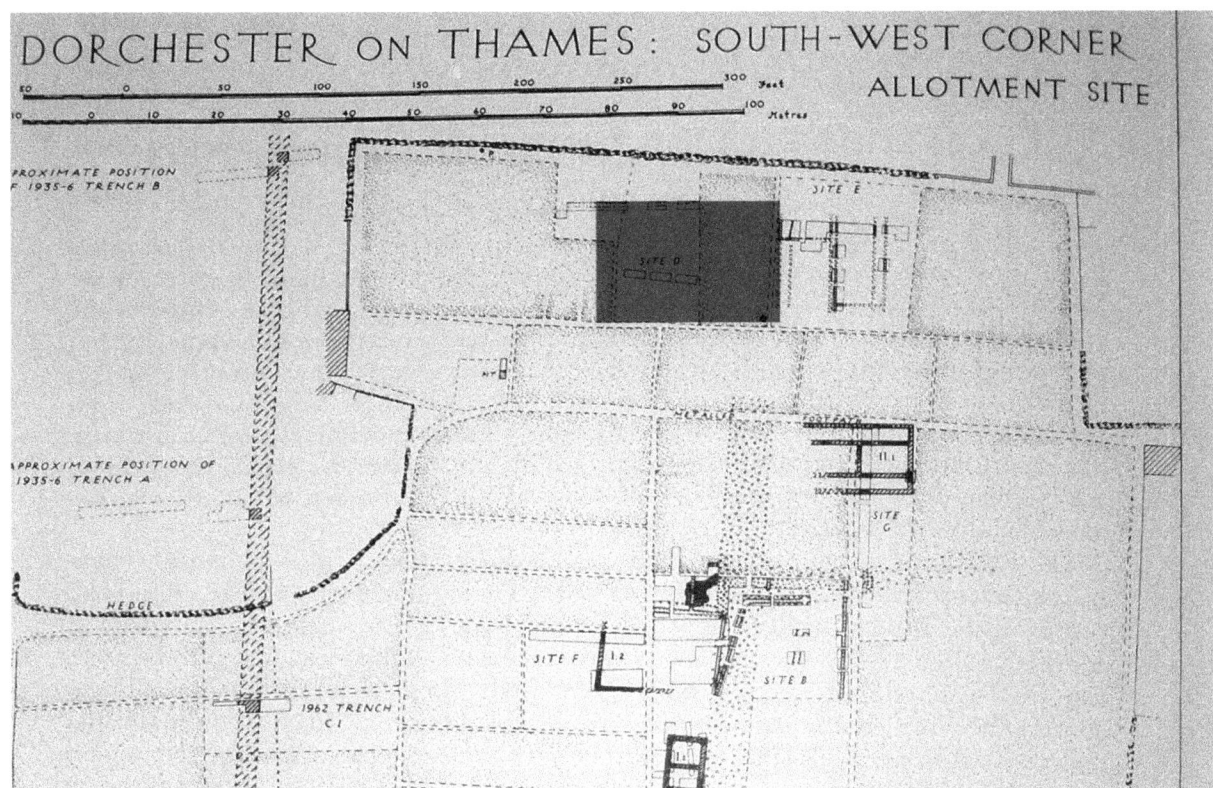

Figure 12. Darkened area indicates approximate location of the 2008 excavation in relation to Frere's 1963 interventions. (after Frere 1984)

In 2007, the first research drive excavation at Dorchester since Frere's fieldwork commenced, as a pilot spearheading what is hoped to be a long-term relationship with the region in terms of survey, excavation, and research. Conducted at the Minchin recreation grounds to the north of the town, the excavation served to extend our knowledge of extramural activity. The following summer, a four-week campaign of survey and excavation took place. Geophysical survey of areas north of the village hinted at the vestigial remains of the Neolithic cursus, once thought completely lost. Magnetometry and resistivity carried out over the northern-most area of the village allotments were less informative, owing to generations of use and re-use during cultivation. The soil had been too much disturbed and there were too many modern intrusions of iron detritus to allow for any significant indications of what was beneath the soil. However, the final three weeks of the digging season were dedicated to revealing in larger frame what Frere could only see through small keyholes. A trench thirty metres square was opened over the same space where Frere has placed several 5-foot slots (Figure 12). At the eastern extremity of the opened area, a north-south Roman road was located. It is likely that this represents the *cardus maximus* or main centre axis road through the heart of the walled town. Into this surface a sub-rectangular feature nearly 2 metres in length was cut. It was initially suspected that this might be a post-Roman grave, but excavation revealed its contents to be largely domestic debris, including a few sherds of early Anglo Saxon pottery among the copious later Roman wares. Additionally, a late Roman key virtually identical to one found in the famous Minchin Recreation post-Roman burial was found within the fill of this 'non-grave' (Figure 13). Less than a metre distant were recovered part of a human cranium and a digit, but given the frequent recovery of human remains in this part of the village, these are more likely to be residual or stray finds than anything related to the grave-shaped feature.

---

[6] The work conducted at 31-32 High street, although inconclusive, exhausted all possibilities in extracting as much information as possible from the site, whilst a bungled watching brief at 14 Watling Lane failed to note that burials had been located on the same site a few years earlier, and missed the opportunity to determine a southern limit to a likely cemetery.

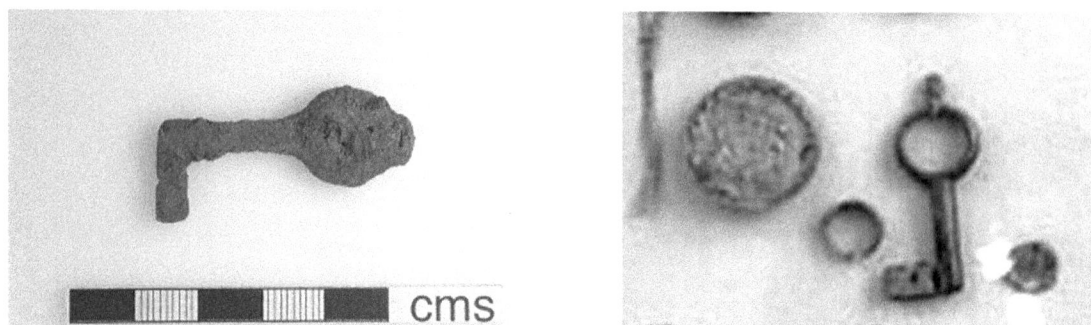

Figure 13. Key recovered from fill of a feature cut into the Roman road surface that appeared to be a grave yet was devoid of human remains (l); key recovered from the female 'Anglo-Saxon' burial north of the village (r)

Figure 14. Copper alloy tripod fixture, 3rd century (l); intaglio depicting Ganymede feeding Jupiter's hawk (r)

The excavation revealed large rubble spreads that seemed to, in some few places, suggest the possibility of structures. These would likely be middle to late Saxon structures, based on their place in the stratigraphy. The short excavation season (three weeks) and the care with which the site was cleaned necessitated backfilling before earlier sequences could be examined, yet the abundance of finds has certainly provided much food for thought in the run-up to the 2009 season. There were very large quantities of later Roman pottery and building material, including some relatively high-status roller-stamp box flue tiles, perhaps from a building previously on or near the excavation site. Perhaps the most exciting small finds were a intaglio of Ganymede feeding Jupiter's hawk and a small cast copper alloy tripod mount of a female head, whose plaited hairstyle suggests a later third century date (Figure 14). Several pin and spoons were also recovered and nearly one hundred coins. In addition to the majority of Roman coins was one 8th century *sceat* (Figure 15), which is an unusual find for Dorchester and tantalising encourages us to hope for more details of that period to emerge. Another unusual find appears to be a silver escutcheon from a 7th century hanging bowl, but as this is still in the conservation process at time of this writing, we can only surmise what this means for interpretation of the site. Although unstratified, the site also produced a zoomorphic belt buckle of Hawkes 1b type, not very unlike that recovered from the Dyke Hills male burial, which is discussed in a further chapter.

Figure 15. 8th century sceat *recovered from the Dorchester allotments*

The following sections will provide a more detailed look at many of the aspects of Roman Dorchester, re-evaluating the old knowledge and incorporating some of the information gained by recent unpublished archived work.

Walls and defences

One of the more hotly contested debates centring on Dorchester has been the placement of the Roman town's defences, specifically the limits of the walled portion of the town (Figure 16). Antiquarians have postulated a variety of dimensions for the town, often citing incorrectly dated evidence. Archaeologists have vacillated, for the last half century at least, between the playing card 'standard' shape for a Roman walled town, and a more creative approach that calls for the incorporation of the River Thame into the scheme as the fourth line of defence. This second hypothesis relies mainly the basis that the higher elevation of the ground upon which the Abbey currently sits would not have been excluded from the walled area. It makes poor defensive strategy to leave such high ground extramural.

When the Oxford University Archaeological Society conducted their preliminary survey of the ramparts of Dorchester in 1935, they clearly defined three of the four lines of the defences, north, west and south. For the eastern limit, they suggested, that based upon settlement cracks appearing in some of the modern buildings, one could justifiably claim the houses were built over the heel of a bank (Stevens and Keeney 1935, 217). They also tentatively stated that it "seemed even possible" (*ibid*) to see the points where this eastern rampart crossed the Oxford-Henley road leading southward away from Dorchester, but that most traces of the eastern rampart "were few and not very satisfactory" (Hogg and Stevens 1937, 44). They wrote that possibly no ditch existed on this side and that "there was some evidence that both north and south ditches ran on beyond the line of the east rampart to join the Thame" (*ibid*, 219). What then could this mean for the later shape of the stone defences?

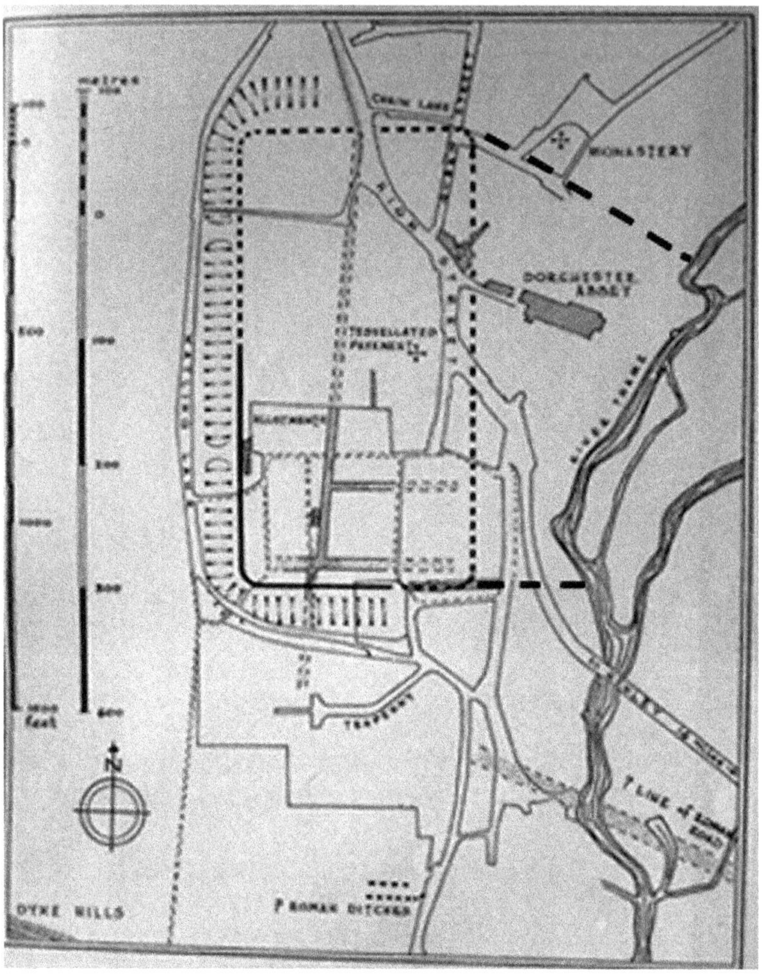

Figure 16. Roman defences – both wall hypotheses marked (after Frere 1962)

In 1962, when a drainage ditch was dug along High Street for the placement of sewer works, a large wall, some 2.5 metres in width (although frustratingly it is not clear if this means thickness or simply the width of the trench) was discovered which, to some, appeared to be incontrovertible evidence of the location of the eastern town wall. Yet this may have been a misinterpretation; in other places along the known wall, robber trenches indicate a lesser dimension of approximately 1.8m (Chambers 1984). This massive wall could have been the stone footings for one of two reported Late Saxon churches in Dorchester, based on the approximate locations as reported by Leland and apparently still visible to observers in the 18th century (Rodwell 2005, 30). Wall thicknesses in excess of 2.5 metres have been noted in some Saxon churches (Heighway and Bryant 1986,191), although arguably there are cases where former Roman town walls have been incorporated into Saxon churches (Kenyon 1948, 8). A discovery of buried human remains in 1844 was reported as "skeletons in the orchard near the Smithy", near the foundations of an "old building" (Manning and Leeds1921, 241). These are marked on the 1887 South Oxfordshire Ordnance Survey map as occurring in the proximity of the wall discovered in 1961, perhaps belonging to the graveyard of one of these churches.

Camden observed, "On the South side of the Church, stood a castle of which there are not the least traces" (Gibson 1695). Naturally, this castle can be discounted as, short of the longevity of name for a nearby public house 'Old Castle', there is no other supporting evidence for there having ever been such an edifice at Dorchester. Yet the implication is that some great stone structure did indeed exist at this southern side of the known abbey. Were is simply a wall, perhaps it might have been described as such, although since it has been suggested that the third century stone improvements to the defences may have included ballista and towers, perhaps it is indeed a bastion on the wall that is represented in the 1961 trench as well as preserved in the local memory at the time of Camden's recording.

One argument in favour of the wall being placed to the west of the Abbey has been made based upon an antiquarian discovery of a cremation burial in the Vicarage Garden in 1866[7] (Harden and Taylor 1939, 293). Based upon the Roman law forbidding burial within town walls, the presence of this solitary cremation has been seen as proof that the area lies outside of the defences. Yet if the mid third century date ascribed to the cremation is correct, then one must accede that the burial itself is already an oddity. Cremation had all but disappeared as part of the Romanised funerary practice by that time in Britain. Surely there must be something exceptional about this burial that was, based on recent excavation in the associated grounds (Keevil 2003, 43) apparently unrelated to any other burials and thus not part of an organised cemetery. Perhaps, while rare, intramural burial was an occasional, exceptional occurrence. The 1997 discovery of a cremation with associated grave goods from Godmanchester provides an interesting parallel. Although somewhat earlier, these cremated remains were located near the centre of the Roman settlement (Taylor 1997, 386), clearly in defiance of the law. As they were the remains of a child, perhaps the law did not apply, yet the inclusion of gold box fittings and numerous pots and clay figures suggests a high-status and highly visible burial rite. The high quality of the decorated glass vessels (Figure 17) that accompanied the Dorchester vicarage garden cremation may also indicate a person of exceptionally high status, for whom the laws may not have applied.

Figure 17. Early third century Roman glass vessels found in the Vicarage Garden in 1866 in association with a cremation burial. (after Cook and Rowley 1985)

Further support for the walls excluding the Abbey comes from a watching brief carried out at 12 High Street in 2002 that recorded a large Roman ditch on a line parallel to that in the west (John Moore Heritage 2002). A later watching brief in 2006 in the property adjacent to Chequers also indicated a northern turn to a ditch that may represent the town defences (John Moore Heritage 2006, 9-10).

---

[7] Plans for the summer of 2009 are underway for a comprehensive geophysical survey of this garden as well as a 1.5m x 1.5m test pit, in part to determine if the 1866 discovery was part of a larger burial ground as well as to increase our understanding of the eastern side of the village, where work has been relatively scant.

Regardless of where the eastern line existed, the strict interpretation of the rectangular shape of the enclosed town is unlikely. In 1972, an excavation of Beech House, near 51 High Street appeared to indicate that the town's later walls and ditches formed a 90-degree angle at the junction of the western and northern defences (Rowley and Brown 1972, 17-18). This conformed neatly with the supposition that the limits of the town were defined by the 'typical' playing card, rectangular shape of Roman small towns. Yet not all excavators in Dorchester at the time agreed with the findings of the Beech House dig, and even eyewitnesses to the excavation felt uncomfortable about some of the conclusions reached (R Bradley, *pers comm*). Indeed, placing the defences at this point marked a severe contrast with the dimensions of the walls and their related banks and ditches along the known western and southern lines, where excavations had shown "that the town wall was separated from the outer ditch by a berm five to eight metres wide" (Chambers 1982, 6).

In 1981, a developer-driven excavation carried out by Oxford Archaeological Unit revealed that the actual defences were in fact several metres to the north of the line previously established. Interestingly, this suggests that the features misinterpreted by the Rowley excavation may represent a hitherto unknown substantial building within the town. Even more germane to the issue of the defences, the alignment of this correctly established wall indicates that the northern line of the wall did not form a right angle with the western side, but rather continued to the northeast, ruling out a strictly rectangular shape for the town. In reality, Roman small towns in Britain seldom exhibited the kind of uniformity associated with fort and camp construction. A sampling of small town shape (Figure 18) indicates that in fact less than 60% of towns in Britain conformed to a pattern of rectilinear defences.

There is arguably enough evidence to consider it likely that the second century defences of Dorchester incorporated the river as a line of defence and therefore included the high ground upon which the abbey now stands. The related outer ditch may even have been kept flooded by allowing the Thame to flow around the town, a suggestion supported by the mollusc data collected from interventions on the western side (Hogg and Stevens 1937, 70-1). Although water table estimations suggest that the river would have been up to three feet below the bottom of the ditch, damming would have easily overcome this, and would not have been beyond Roman engineering abilities. At Cirencester, the bridge outside the Verulamium gate implies a design to divert the river to run outside the defences (Wacher 1966, 66). But even if one concedes that the ramparts and ditch defence followed this path, what can we say of the third century stone walls? It does not necessarily follow that the limits of the town set in stone were identical to the earlier earthworks. Although it is evident that they do coincide along three of the four cardinal lengths, there is no reason to rule out the possibility that the third century stone fortifications may have enclosed a smaller space, either for reasons of economy or function. If the

Figure 18. Comparative sizes and shapes of Roman town defences in Britain (after Burnham 1988)

function of the wall was to convey status rather than to provide protection, then leaving the raised contour where the abbey now sits outside of the walled space need not have been considered a liability.

Nothing short of a series of interventions across the projected line of the eastern wall will settle the debate for all. One can easily be pulled from pillar to post and back again by the arguments and interpretations on either side. Most importantly, one must ask the question: what will resolving the wall debate *really* tell us about Roman Dorchester? Indeed, it is more than simply a matter of who has the correct line on map. Our understanding of the internal arrangements of the town is directly affected by our knowledge of what constituted the internal space. Determining where the walled defences were located may help us to establish gate locations, and form a clearer picture of the function of these defences. Were they constructed in the face of some threat of violence or attack, or were they a monumental statement of the town's perceived status?

Dorchester's Altar

For the antiquarian enthusiasts of Roman Britain, one of the more frustrating voids in the material evidence was the lack of epigraphy from the Oxfordshire region in general, and in Dorchester specifically. Despite all the early references to ruins and artefacts, there was still not one shred of inscription in the area. Then, in 1731, an altar[8] was recovered, much to the excitement of the local antiquarians (Figure 19).

One eyewitness, a Mr. Fisher, recorded the discovery in his diary (Harden and Taylor 1939, 295). Subsequent reports have placed its find spot behind the Red Lion Inn (near present High Street), during the construction of a saw pit at a depth of 5 ft (*ibid*, 294), at the site of the vicarage (Crake 1889,311) at a depth of 12 ft, or in the Hemp Croft (Gough 1806, 28). The timing of the discovery was indeed serendipitous as John Horsley's volume *Britannia Romana* was nearly set for publication, and he was able to add this unique inscription to the book.

The inscription is generally translated as reading "To Jupiter Optimus Maximus and the spirits of the Augusti, Marcus Varius Severus set up this altar with rails (screens) at his own expense". These types of dedications, jointly made to Jupiter Optimus Maximus and the *numina* of the Emperor[s], were in almost all cases "made corporately by detachments" or entire military units (Fishwick 1961, 214). In the Dorchester altar, we have a rare example of an individual making a traditionally group dedication. This may explain the *de suo posuit* inclusion, since his particular choice of dedication might otherwise have been interpreted to indicate an expenditure footed by an entire group of men; M. Severus would have wanted to be certain that the recognition of such a pious act benefited him solely.

The stone was removed by the local magistrate, Sir Henry Oxenden, who eventually relocated the altar to his gardens in Kent, at Broome Park. Of the modern scholars, only Haverfield was able to examine it at the close of the nineteenth century, and even he, rather than travel to the site, sent a student to produce a rubbing for him to examine. Naturally, it would be preferable to be able to cast a modern critical eye over the original, but when the last heir to the Estate, Sir Percy Dixwell-Oxenden sold the property to Lord Kitchener of Khartoum in 1909, the altar disappeared. Its last documented appearance was in the background of a cover photograph of the June 1907 edition of *Country Living*, too far removed from the camera to make out any detail. It is assumed that the altar was either moved or given away by Dixon-Oxenden before the sale, or by Kitchener during his infamous re-designing of the estate.

An attempt to locate it in the 1930s (Collingwood 1965, 76), involving an appeal for information in the London Times as well as letters of enquiry sent to surviving members of the Oxenden family, met with no success.[9] A more recent attempt by this author, involving a search through the Kitchener archive and the former estates of the Oxenden family has, as yet, been equally fruitless.

---

[8] *RIB* 235

[9] Letters of response to the enquiries made by D.B. Harden and M.V. Taylor, with reference to the Feb 25, 1938 London Times advertisement, are located in the Dorchester-on-Thames documentary archive (Box 3) at the Ashmolean Museum.

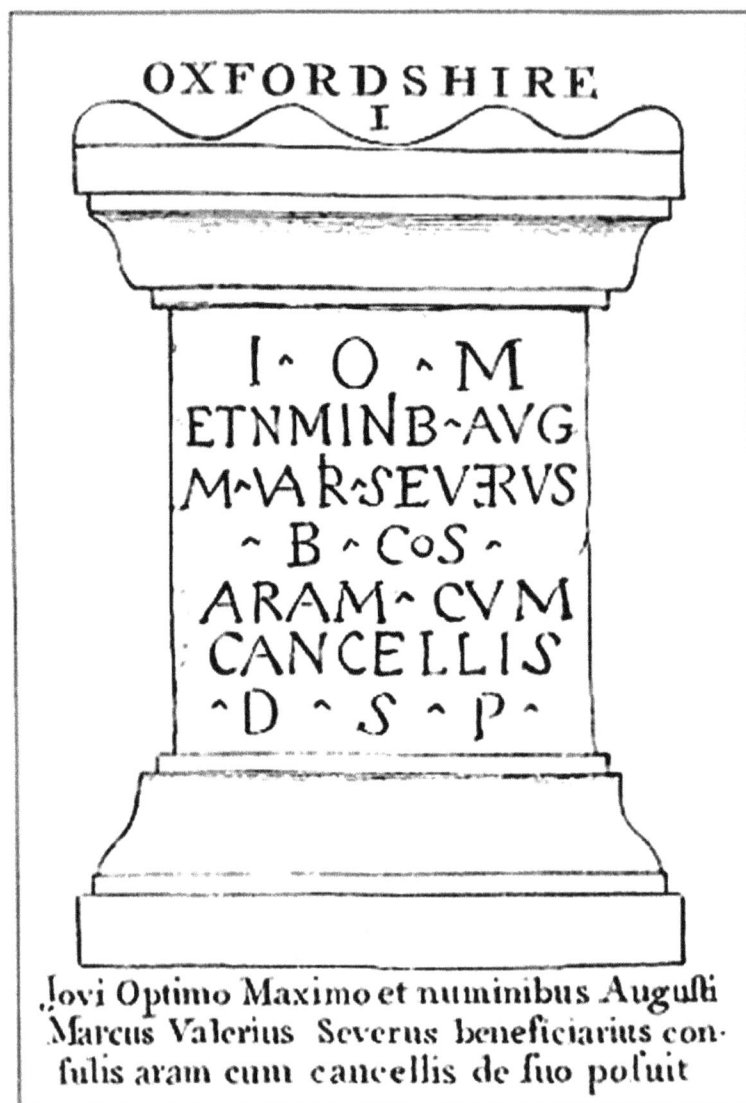

Figure 19. The Dorchester Altar (after Horsley 1732)

One may argue that locating the altar is of little academic importance, since we have the 1731 sketch. However, given that so many assumptions about the role Dorchester played in the Roman occupation and administration of Britain are based upon the interpretation of this solitary find; it might be helpful if we could submit the item to modern examination and validation in order to rule out the possibility of false evidence. The manor house at Elsfield produced a similar altar[10] around 1750, a fake produced for Bodleian librarian and antiquarian Francis Wise. Curiously, only the Elsfield fake and the Dorchester altar exhibit the **B Cos** abbreviation for a *beneficiarius consularis*, where all other known examples prefer **B F Cos** (Goodburn and Waugh 1983, 59). Traditionally explained as the influence of the genuine Dorchester altar over the creation of the forgery, perhaps it could be viewed as the signature of fraud on both items. Collingwood records nearly a dozen forged inscriptions in Britain that appeared in the first half of the eighteenth century (1965). Admittedly unlikely, the possibility remains that the fortuitous appearance of the Dorchester altar could be viewed with some suspicion. One must remember the Richard of Cirencester Itinerary, validated by no less an authority on the ancient than Stukely, was later proven to be false. Without the altar to examine we must rely solely on antiquarian reports.

One of the great perils of following the antiquarian trail is that very early works such as Leland, Camden and Hearne, have been so often edited, collated and revised in the nineteenth and twentieth

---

[10] *RIB* 2336

centuries that they are altered greatly, like a game of Chinese whispers. For example, Gough relates the sale of the Dorchester altar to Lord Oxenden for the price of a guinea (1806, 28). Hearne tells us in his diary of the night when a police Constable had to be summoned to Dorchester to keep the peace after a riot broke out when a "gentleman of Sandwich" attempted to purchase the Stone for a guinea. Lord Oxenden's men prevented this and removed the altar to his lordship's kitchen for safekeeping (Salter 1915, 438). Hearne had much else to add about the altar in his diaries; he was very excited about the discovery, but when he received a copy of the inscription he remarked "I much suspected the said copy and not without reason" (*ibid*, 428) citing later that he had never met with the word *cancelli* in any old inscription, nor had his colleagues (436). He finds it curious that his acquaintance Mr Beckett, a friend of Stukely, should deny any knowledge of the altar on two separate occasions and not wish to speak of it. (451).

There is seemingly enough evidence to produce a reasonable suspicion of authenticity; recovering the altar is the only way to be completely certain.[11] However, if the altar were authentic as tradition states, it would be helpful to know more about its origin. Although assumed by some to have been carved from Cotswold oolitic limestone and brought down the Thames (Henig and Booth 2000, 116), those who examined it in 1731 believed it originated in the Headington Quarry (Salter 1915, 447), and thus would have travelled over land. How far it travelled and how costly that is likely to have been could tell us much about the influence and wealth of the man who caused it to be erected and what the presence of this *beneficiarius* meant to the settlement.

It is important to understand the role of the *beneficiarius consularis* within the larger context of the Empire, for only then can one determine not only the significance of such a person's presence in Dorchester, but also perhaps the level of imperial involvement in the smaller towns of the Britain. Regrettably, the very title is vague enough to have allowed for a variety of interpretation. We can be certain that those bestowed with the title were 'chosen men' but the exact duties they would have been expected to carry out likely varied across the range of place and time within the Empire. Iconographic evidence from mortuary stones suggest that the primary function of a *beneficiarius consularis* involved the use of scroll and stylus (Dise 1995, 76), yet it is likely that they were more than elevated yeomen. It has been suggested that a major function of provincial *beneficiarii* was to monitor traffic on roads, a model bolstered by study of the number of dedicated altars along major nets of roads across the Empire (von Domaszewski 1902, 210-11). However, scholars have offered different arguments for the primary function to have been variously the regular policing of the *cursus publicus* (Pflaum 1940, 147), collection and organisation of the *annona* (MacMullen 1963, 56), or the pacification of conflict arising from discontented provincial populations (MacMullen 1966, 260). It is likely that these officials were "generalists" (Dise 1995, 80), stationed on their own and performing a variety of administrative duties that were largely imperial as opposed to local functions, implying that in these smaller towns, "imperial presence was modest at best" (*ibid*)

The desire to see the altar as part of a greater structure fed the imaginations of such observers as Hearne, who imagined a grand temple at Dorchester, where he speculated the Dobunni had their capital (Salter 1915, 440). Later indications showed Dobunnic capital likely to have been instead at Cirencester, although the pitfalls of trying to force "tribal" identities, boundaries and capitals upon the pre-Roman Iron Age occupants of Southern Britain have been alluded to in the previous chapter. The description *aram cum cancellis* indicates an altar with screens, or more likely, rails, given the later Christian church use of altar railings perhaps hinting at earlier pagan origins. Thus, we can perhaps imagine an altar with ornate stone railings separating it from the profane space around it. Hearne's contemporaries believed it to be an altar for prayer rather than sacrifices, given its lack of a physical focus (Salter 1915, 447). Accordingly, it would not necessarily have to have belonged in a larger structure, but may have been a free-standing altar more in keeping with the modest nature of the town.

The M. Severus altar is not the sole evidence we have for the existence and persistence of religious and ritual activity in Roman Dorchester. Indeed, beyond the ostentatious (and perhaps questionable)

---

[11] The possibility of fakery was discussed with Dr Martin Henig; although he believes the altar to have been authentic, primarily based upon the style of inscription indicated in the 1731 sketch, he concurred that finding the stone, in the absence of even the Haverfield rubbing to examine, would be useful and indeed would completely eradicate any doubts.

dedication of stone, there were many other forms of ritual behaviour occurring in the settlement that shall be discussed in the next section.

Ritual and religion in Roman Dorchester

Without a clear understanding of the entire internal arrangements of the town, and in the absence of any known public buildings, it is difficult to make definitive statements about the nature of formalised religious activity that may have taken place in Dorchester during the first to fourth centuries AD. Yet some tantalising clues may indicate that both contemporary "Romanised" observances as well as remnant native rituals were taking place in and around the settlement. The previously mentioned altar of M. Severus clearly suggests the practice of public worship and perhaps sacrifices to at least the chief of the Roman gods and to the cult of the emperor. But what other evidence exists for ritual activity in Dorchester?

One of the previously mentioned factors in the defences debate is the position of the high ground where the current medieval abbey is located. It is always tempting to engage the eye of imagination to see a continuity of sacred space at that site, assuming that the citizens of Roman Dorchester had a temple or sanctuary there. Logistically, it is a compelling thought, as many other temple locations in Southern England tend to be located on higher elevations and intramural temples are well represented (Lewis 1966). Undoubtedly, the proximity of the Thame would make the spot a visually appealing prospect for the placement of a temple, but there has been no material evidence to suggest that any such structure ever existed at this location. Alternatively, the location may have been left out of the defences in spite of its elevation because it already housed a temple/ mortuary complex that should not be included in the walled town (Rodwell 2005, 20). Certainly, given that the spot was the likely location of St Birinus' Saxon Church, followed by the later medieval structure that exists in its modified form today, the materials that may have made up the structure of a temple or shrine could have been robbed out, reused and carted away. Excavations in advance of the installation of a boiler system for the abbey revealed no sign of any Roman features (Keevil, 2003) but the interventions were small and certainly not exhaustive. Renovations during the nineteenth century at the Abbey revealed that in "digging down 12 feet a Roman pavement" was dug through and under it the remains of burnt corn and bones were found (Manning and Leeds 1921, 241). A significant number of coloured *tesserae* found in 2001 (Keevil 2003, 344-5) have been interpreted as possibly belonging to a temple or mausoleum (Rodwell 2005, 20), supported by the finds of an Iron Age gold stater and the two Roman brooches, one with enamel inlays (Keevil 2003, 353; Cunningham and Banks 1972, 158), common devotional deposits at ritual sites.

It would not be unusual for a town to have more than one temple or shrine. At 1 Samian Way, a 1992 evaluation pit dug in advance of a foundation construction revealed nearly a heavy concentration of first century potsherds, but also a surprisingly high number of bird bones (Oxford Archaeology 1992, 3). Birds are not traditionally well represented on sites, and it is tempting to see these longitudinally split bird bones as the debris leftover from sacrifices. The role of birds in Romano-British ritual has "perhaps been understated" (Parker 1988, 206) and it is not impossible to consider this unusual deposit suggestive of a religious focus. This site revealed " a complex series of archaeological features likely to be of the early Roman period in a fair state of preservation beginning at 0.70m below grade" (Oxford Archaeology 1992, 4), significantly higher in elevation than comparable dated contexts elsewhere in the town. The 2007 excavation in Haven Close also revealed early period artefacts and a complex series of ditches. This general area south of the town has often been commented on for its peculiar rise in elevation, and indeed antiquarians often believed the roughly circular area of elevation to be indicative of an amphitheatre, an unfounded claim, but one that draws attention to the anomaly in elevation. As has been mentioned previously, elevated areas near towns were often preferred sites for temples, shrines and places of ritual focus. The Roman temple at Jordan Hill, Weymouth exhibited a large amount of bird bones and coins in deliberately repeated sequences (Manning 1972, 247). Perhaps the high percentage of coins found in the south of Dorchester may support the suggestion of a ritual focus at or near this site.

In the absence of firmer evidence for a temple at Dorchester, we must look at other expressions of ritual activity. Coin hoards may have had ritual purpose and served as votive offerings, particularly the later Roman deposits of "worthless" denominations, many of which had been out of circulation for some time (Aitchison 1988, 277). Within the relatively small confines of the 1962-3 excavations, three separate late fourth century coin hoards, totalling 857 coins were recovered (Reece 1984, 132-3). As seen from the antiquarian reports, coins have been turning up in Dorchester at least since the sixteenth century, and the near ubiquitous presence of coins in the soils may relate to scattering of hoards through disturbance and ploughing rather than through accidental coin loss, suggesting that perhaps the town was not so much a hub of economic activity, but rather a focus for religious cultic activity. It has been suggested that the Dorchester coins were, based upon their excellent condition, kept out of general circulation, suggesting they may have been kept as keepsakes or curios, and that there is the implication that the keeping of old coins was a "local habit" not typical in hoards of this type elsewhere (Reece 1984, 133). This is particularly significant in that it may mean that the earlier coins discovered around Dorchester could be attributed to the latest period of coin usage in the town.

Aitchison links some votive coin offerings with other metalwork deposits, both in Iron Age and Romano-British contexts (1988, 279), and indeed coins were not the only objects being hoarded at Dorchester. The 1962 excavations in the allotments (Frere 1962, 119) revealed a hoard of iron implements buried in the silting that had accumulated at the rear of the bank forming the southern rampart (Figure 11). The hoard was dated to the late fourth century and contained Roman farming gear including a ploughshare, coulter, mortice chisel, and a socketed spud for weeding as well as less function-specific items such as bucket fittings, a bolt plate and nails (Manning 1984, 139-147). This deliberate ritual deposit of iron implements, particularly faming equipment such as ploughshares, is an occurrence seen over and over again in the later Iron Age, with examples from Frilford (Bradford and Goodchild 1939, 13), Harlow, Essex (Bartlett 1988) and Hod Hill (Richmond 1968, 19-22) among others. Placement of such deposits within the tail of earthen ramparts is seen at Madmarston Camp, Oxfordshire and at South Cadbury (Manning 1984, 142), and the similarities may be significant. Hingley compiled a gazetteer of sites where iron objects were deposited in the later pre-historic and Roman periods and there are two major periods into which these types of tool hoards fall: Late Iron Age and third-fourth century Roman (2006, 241-51). It is suggested that perhaps there were "links with the past", that some ritual behaviour exhibited in Roman Britain was pervasive (Fulford 2001), an atavistic performance of votive depositions. The possible greater significance of this return to pre-Roman traditions will be discussed in more depth further on.

Fulford's work on pervasive ritual also indicates that at Silchester, wells were commonly used for more than their primary purpose and indeed many feature interpreted as wells, despite the absence of evidence of any stone or timber lining, may have been dug for other purposes (Fulford 2001, 201). At Dorchester, an excavation was carried out from 1960 to 1962 by the Oxford University Archaeological Society, intent on learning more about the medieval cloister and surrounding structures at the Abbey (Cunningham and Banks 1972, 158-164). These excavations revealed a rectangular Roman well containing a large quantity of late first century pottery. Fulford notes that a "common denominator" for many of these deliberate deposit wells is the presence of "one or more complete or near complete pottery vessels" (2001, 202). The Abbey well contained many examples, perhaps suggesting a ritual function, although Young suggests that the high number of wasters present in the assemblage may indicate the presence of a kiln on site and that the well was simply used as a dump (Frere 1984, 128-9).

In the centre of the allotments, a fragment of a jet panel was found, showing a hand and upraised arm, similar to those that depict seated male deities, (Frere 1984, 139). This fragment was interpreted as likely being a casket decoration, although it may have belonged to a devotional altar for household gods. Additionally, sherds were recovered from the southern central part of the allotments (Frere 1963, 139) from a fine hard orange-ware vessel with a cream slip depicting a female figure (Figure 20), characteristic of vessels associated with ritual use. Two other known examples of this type also depict birds and snakes and are associated with religious activity (Behrens 1954, 111-2).

Figure 20. Sherds from ritual flagon (l); hoard of iron implements (Frere 1962)

The long-standing operation and apparent success of pagan religious centres in the region such as the complex at Frilford and the temple and fairground at Woodeaton indicate that even in the late fourth century, when Christianity was the nominative the religion of the Empire, it had far from supplanted and indeed perhaps simply supplemented the practice of traditional beliefs. The indigenous population had become quite adept at incorporating their own deities into foreign belief frameworks, such as the alignment of 'Celtic' gods and goddesses with the Roman pantheon. Therefore it would be unsurprising to see a similar effect when Christianity crossed the channel. At nearby Long Wittenham, a child's burial with a beaker decorated with images from biblical stories has been interpreted as a Christian grave in spite of the inclusion of grave goods. The beaker may also be seen as a pagan grave good included not for the importance of the stories depicted, but for the significance of the craftsmanship and display of skill indicated by the repoussé images. At both Hinton St Mary and Frampton (Dorset), mosaics depict the Chi Rho and the bust of Christ along side pagan elements. This has been interpreted as the reduction of the pagan deities to mere allegory, used to illustrate the Christian message (Toynbee 1968, 182-4), but it is perhaps more likely that for many, the new Christ was incorporated into the extant framework of religious belief.

Although the literary evidence exists for a complex and learned ecclesiastical society in Britain by the late fourth and early fifth centuries, the archaeological evidence is scant. Much is made of the organised and vigorous destruction of many Mithraea, implying the righteous fury of a Christian population. However, Watson (1968, 53) provides an alternative explanation, where common soldiers of any faith would relish the chance to destroy what had for the most part been the ritual preserve of senior officers. The literature cannot be ignored, but it is likely that the segment of the population that was engaged in the great debates over heresy and other "ecclesiastical disputes" (Frend 1968, 44) was rather small and restricted to wealthy estate owners and urbanites. In a small town such as Dorchester, the influence of Christianity is assumed rather than proved based on several late Roman cemeteries that exhibit such traditionally understood characteristics of the Christian burial rite as east-west alignment and a lack of grave goods. However, a closer look at the Queensford Mill cemetery (Figure 21) highlights an interesting coincidence. The apparent east west alignment is, when examined more thoroughly, not east-west at all. Figure 21 shows the alignment of the burials in relation to the alignment of the Neolithic cursus, the terminus of which is at the Queensford Mill cemetery.

Admittedly, is uncertain if this part of the cursus was still recognisable in the landscape during the time of the Roman occupation (G Hey, *pers comm*) although the Drayton North cursus was respected by a Roman enclosure, suggesting that at least some of these Neolithic features were apparent to the inhabitants during the Roman period (Barclay *et al* 2003, 107-8). The site yielded some third century sherds and the radiocarbon dates for the establishment of the cemetery allow for a range beginning AD 320, but this was discounted due to the supposed Christian alignment and the lack of grave goods (Durham and Rowley 1973, 37). However, if respect for this monument guided the alignment decision in this cemetery then perhaps the assumption that the graves belong to a *completely* Christian tradition is misleading.

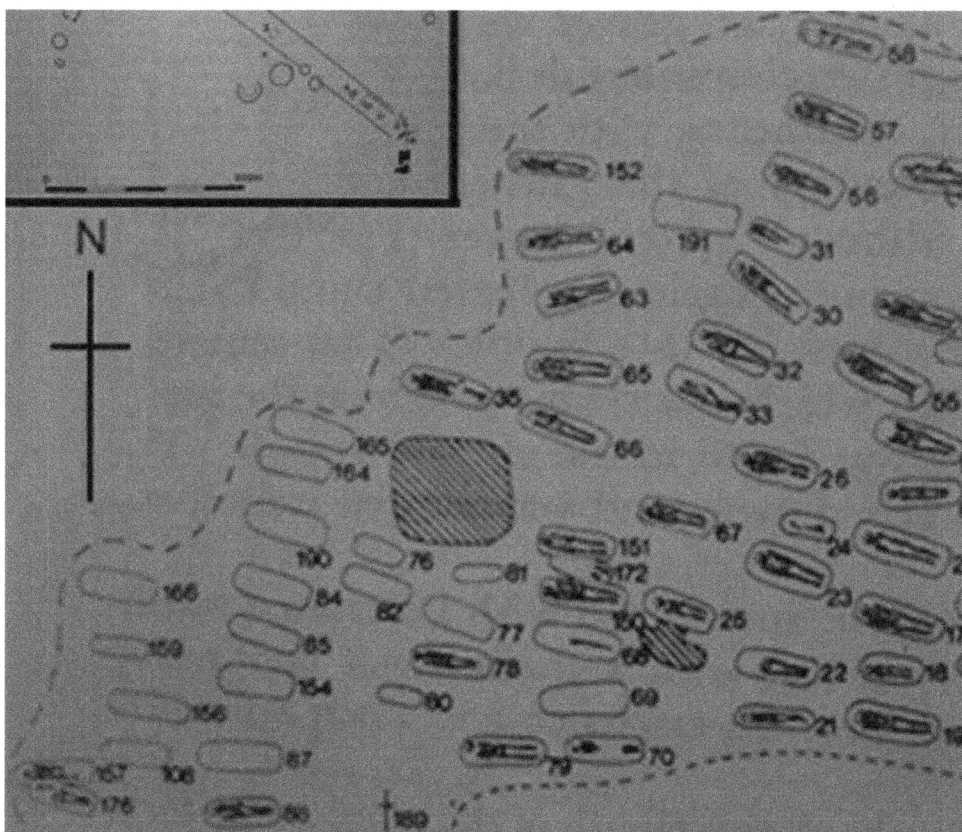

Figure 21. Queenford Cemetery with (inset) cursus alignment
(after Durham and Rowley 1972; Whittle et al *1992)*

Indeed, this would not be the only example at Dorchester of Christian activity being guided by pre-Christian practice, as the alignment of Dorchester Abbey, existing as it does over the likely footprint of the earliest church, is not strictly east-west either, but more than 20 degrees off, following the more north-westerly alignment of a pair of ditches which may have formed a boundary "already fossilised in the landscape and even older than the Roman town" (Rodwell 2005, 27). A curious side note to this observation is found in the recent research conducted on the orientation of churches. Over 1500 churches in Britain were recorded with regard to their orientation in an attempt to settle the debate about whether or not church alignment was based upon the location of true east or on the sunrise location on the feast day of the church's patron. The results, which handily debunked the folkloric patron saint idea, also indicated that while very few churches are actually on an true east-west alignment, it is apparent that there was "a clear intention" to align the buildings roughly to the east (Hinton 2006, 223).

If the beliefs and ritual practices of the inhabitants of the area had mutated into a pagan-Christian amalgam, then this alone may have been reason enough for Birinus to choose the settlement for his ministry. The practice of co-opting local ritual preference in order to secure Christianisation was a well-exploited tactic and might explain the anomalous orientation of the Abbey. Dorchester's role as a ritual centre is clearly significant; however there is as yet too much uncertainty to suggest a 'ritual continuity' over several millennia.

Dorchester's Roman fort

One of the pillars of Roman studies in Britain has been the belief in the omnipresence of forts across the entire extent of Roman influence. Some scholars believe that "almost all towns and small settlements occupied sites adjacent to earlier forts" (Webster 1966, 32), the usual pattern involving a *vicus* that grew up eventually into the small town or smaller city. It is often believed that if there was a significant settlement, a fort must have been present (Frere, *pers comm*), even if the substantiating evidence is specious. Yet as far back as the 1920's some were offering a voice of dissent. Haverfield allowed that scholars incorrectly viewed Britain as "perpetually resounding to the tramp of the mail-clad legionary" (Haverfield and MacDonald 1924, 152), and in fact argued that for much of the period, the 'lowlands' of England, including the Thames Valley, contained virtually no troops and that the only representation of a military nature in the region was that of the commissariat and transport officers, as possibly indicated at Dorchester by the previously mentioned *beneficiarius*.

The presence of Tiberio-Claudian imports in the primary occupation layer of the 1962 allotment excavations has been explained by Frere as belonging to a native settlement that sprang up beside a Claudian fort, although he acknowledged "such a fort is not yet attested" (1964, 129) In her recent history of the Dorchester Abbey, Tiller writes "surprisingly little is known of the fort" (2005, 11). There may be a Gordian solution to this puzzle, but before dismissing the Dorchester fort entirely, we must examine the few pieces of evidence that speak in its favour. Frere referred to "suggestive crop marks yet to be investigated" to the south of the village (Frere 1964, 129) but admittedly, these seem fairly scant marks upon which to base a fort, particularly in light of the fact that they had not been more closely examined and in 1984 Frere reported that as the marks had not been recurrent they were likely agricultural in origin. Frere felt his fort was vindicated when his 1963 excavation in the northern part of the allotments located what were interpreted as first century military timber buildings (Frere 1984, 95). There is no good reason why they could not be a form of civilian dwelling.

Fitting Dorchester into the broader context of Conquest-era southern Britain, while retaining an understanding of the likely native openness to continental influence in the region, requires a willingness to explore alternatives. Creighton (2006, 67) writes of the early timber buildings at Silchester: "By assuming the building must be post AD 43, are we closing our minds to potential evidence for pre-Claudian contact or military influence"? Certainly, given the previously mentioned Silchester evidence for the establishment of a pre-Claudian trading post or the continental example of Magdalensberg in Noricum, in the years prior to subjugation, one could visualise a Dorchester open to Roman trade, home to a few continental traders and their Roman style timber structures and, when the time came, open to Roman occupation.

Frere also suggested that the peculiar nature of the north-south street plan in the town might indicate a fort. Based upon the engineering calculations of Hargreaves *et al* (1978, 6) who projected the probable line of the Roman road from the river crossing, established the most likely spot for the fort (Figure 22), the Old Castle Inn excavations should have provided corroborating evidence. However, Bradley (1978, 36) saw no evidence of this and decided that the first buildings on the site post-dated the defences.

Some support for a fort may be indicated by Frere's demolition layer; the entire area, both within the extent of Frere's excavation, and at the Old Castle site to the east, exhibits a clay deposit of made ground, nearly one metre thick in some places, that seals the first century material and features. This could have been laid down after the deliberate destruction of the fort, in order to establish a *tabula rasa*, set for a completely fresh civilian direction for the town's subsequent growth. Such a pattern is not entirely unheard of, and is best represented by the razing and re-building of Viriconium (Jones and Mattingly 1990, 168). Yet it would not be impossible for a similar restructuring to have taken place after the troubles of the AD 60s regardless of the presence or absence of a fort at Dorchester.

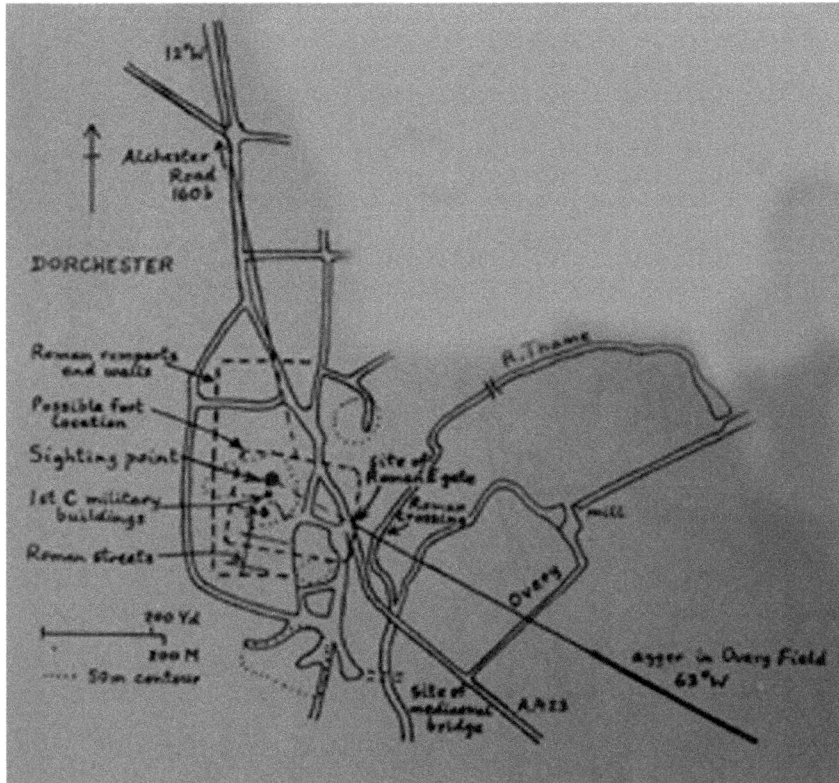

Figure 22. Likely fort location based on Frere's interpretation, projected road lines and application of presumed Roman engineering practices. (Hargreaves et al 1978)

Some believe that the most conclusive evidence for a fort at Dorchester is the coin pattern, which indicates from analogous sites a military presence (P Booth, *pers comm*). Yet the coin evidence indicates that if a fort was present at Dorchester, it could not have been there prior to 60AD and therefore was not a place of chief strategic importance for the conquest of southern Britain (Booth *et al* 2007, 45). The pottery assemblage from Haven Close may be as early as AD 50 (P Booth *pers comm*), and the general strength of the early assemblages, particularly in the south of the village, indicates a strong open settlement that would predate the supposed fort. It may be instead that a community lived here that was already friendly to Roman interests and utilised Roman commodities.

By the beginning of the first century AD, the indigenous Britons were well into a process of social change that led to settlement nucleation (Cunliffe 2005, 601). Of the known Roman small towns in the 'urbanised' zone of the south and east, some 45% have definite or probable Iron Age predecessors, with only 23% having a military origin (Burnham 1986, 193). This suggests that there may have been a greater native agency to the location of a larger settlement at Dorchester, which does not require the presence of a fort to explain.

Extramural activity

Outside of the town defences, the surrounding countryside was far from empty. To the north of the ramparts, there has been much evidence from development-led work to indicate that the town was surrounded by farmland and homesteads. At Mount Farm, Dorchester, there is environmental evidence of extensive celery growth (Robinson 1992, 58) suggesting a specialisation in crop type, serving perhaps as market garden for the town. Animal enclosures and ditched land boundaries are most prevalent, dating from the second to the fourth centuries. At the Minchin Recreation Ground, a series of square enclosures visible from aerial photographs were confirmed in a 2007 research excavation to be third to fourth century animal enclosures, one containing a waterhole, which had steps, built into the side to facilitate the animals reaching the water.

Figure 23. Pots reportedly recovered from north of the Minchin recreation Ground (above), according to a note accompanying the photograph in the Ashmolean Museum archive and pots found in the attic of a Dorchester resident (below). Note the similarity in the breakage lines suggesting they are the same vessels. (upper photograph courtesy Ashmolean Museum; lower, courtesy John Metcalfe)

The Beech House site within the northwestern defences, yielding large quantities of butchered animal bone and horn core (Grant 1981, 53) indicates the importance of the animal processing in third-fourth century Dorchester, and how the extramural enclosures may have supported this industry. A few earlier second century domestic finds at this site indicate that the area had been in use for some time, and the presence of glass sherds, a sherd from fine moulded face flagon[12] and a stylus indicate a higher status domicile in the vicinity. It is worth noting that prior to its being rendered into a gravel quarry to aid the war effort during the 1940's, crop marks and trackways were noted in the adjoining field, and a large intact urn recovered from that site.

In Farm Field, just north of the Minchin Recreation Ground, samian ware and fragments of tile were found in 1928 in what are described as "habitation pits" (Harden and Taylor 1939, 243), similarly indicative of an associated dwelling. Earlier, in 1911 a landowner in this same Farm Field reported via a note to the keeper of the Ashmolean Museum that he had discovered a group of intact pots. A photograph of the collection (Figure 23) accompanying the note documents the finds. Curiously, in the autumn of 2008, an elderly resident of Dorchester discovered several vessels in her attic and recalled that in her youth she had excavated these and others from her father's field, located much closer to the northern line of the defences. Either way, the quality of the pots suggests that they were relatively high status items from the mid second century and may have accompanied a cremation burial (P Booth, *pers comm*). In light of the famous Minchin burial from the same area as the location first indicated for the recovery of the pots, one might be tempted to see a longevity of burial usage; however, as the second proposed findspot is also along the road leading from the north into the village, either spot is equally likely to have been used for prominent burials.

An evaluation at 11 Queen's Lane revealed a rectangular pit, that appeared to be stone lined, but the archive contains neither fill descriptions nor associated finds and the existent site plan was re-sketched from notes and slides after the original was lost. Potentially this could have been an interesting site to determine intra/extramural activities, but as it stands, it must only feed speculation. Another assessment carried out at   27 Martin's Lane was far more useful and provided evidence of "at least one stone founded building" standing on the site with traces of a cobbled yard surface (Chambers 1986, 2). Although no high status villa has been found in close proximity to the walled town, there was certainly no lack of successful farmsteads. In 2004 a watching brief conducted by John Moore Heritage Services reported that no Roman material of any kind had surfaced at 8 Wittenham Lane, suggesting that there was no Roman activity this far south of the town. Yet a 2007 excavation in Haven Close lane produced a prodigious amount of occupational debris, including a vast amount (for the size of the intervention) of extremely early pottery (pre-Flavian). Thames Valley Archaeology Services located in that same area an inhumation with associated pottery from a similarly early date (TVAS 2008). Additionally, an infant burial radiocarbon dated to the fourth century was found at a relatively shallow depth. This indicates that indeed there was Roman activity going on to the south of the settlement, perhaps highly active during the pre-rampart stage when there was an open settlement here, which remained a site of extramural habitation after the fortification of the town.

Later Roman changes

Following the re-organisation of the defences of Dorchester, building and maintenance of the substantial structures were still ongoing. Frere's excavations indicated that the latest structure confirmed to have been constructed in the allotments, was erected sometime after the issuing of a coin of Honorius (394-5), which was found under the foundations in nearly perfect condition. The slender stone footing of this building, suggesting it was half timbered, along with indications of contemporary fully timbered buildings nearby, indicated to Frere that they must represent the simple housing of a military force garrisoned at Dorchester (Frere 1966, 94). The work at the Old Castle Inn and at Beech House sites also indicate that later fourth century structures were conforming to the lighter, less stone intensive pattern.

---

[12] Young Type C11

In spite of the growing number of substantial Roman structures indicated in the archaeological record of Dorchester, we still know very little about their functions and what their role in the settlement may have been. Todd (1970, 115) suggests that it required much more than walled defences to make a settlement a town. Although certain public amenities as would have been common in the Mediterranean were likely to have been luxuries largely dependent upon private munificence, and thus perhaps explaining their absence in some small towns of Britain, there were some features that would have been considered indispensable in order to even consider a settlement 'urban'. The most crucial of these was "the presence of buildings which represented that truly urban characteristic, government, public order, and corporate life" (*ibid*). The absence of such structures as a forum, temple precinct or basilica from Dorchester may be simply the product of the limits imposed upon excavation, but there is also the very real chance that such structures never existed here, and the appellation 'town' is one no Roman would ever have given to the place.

Reece (1980) maintains that by the fourth century, the role of the small town had so changed from what it was in the second century, that both the towns and their surrounding rural homesteads would have been profoundly affected (78). The intensity of the Romanisation of Britain was not as great as in other parts of the Empire, Reece argues, and he even likens it to an "unsuccessful transfusion of Romanitas" (85). Thus Late Roman Britain was Roman by right of ownership, but perhaps less so by way of influence, causing the arrangements of town and country life to undergo a change.

By 350, change was going on at Dorchester. This was not the continuity of the same type of town, but rather a new expression of a people reacting as best they could to the changes raging in the larger world around them. Some indication of this great change can be seen at the Beech House site, where lime-kilns are cut into the existing residence and likely fed from the very stone and mortar of the structures around them (Rowley and Brown 1981, 8). The Old Castle site revealed a plastered wall, brightly painted that collapsed and was left un-repaired (Bradley 1978, 32). A late fourth century building in the allotments, with evidence of richly coloured *tesserae*, was allowed to become ruinous, but was later possibly repaired (Frere 1984, 116). Ritual activity may have taken a different turn with the rise of hoard deposition, as discussed above.

At the end of the fourth century, the changes in the rest of the Roman Empire had to have been affecting at least the economic life of her northern provinces, and both cities and small towns, at the economic centres of their spheres, felt the brunt of it. The smaller towns like Dorchester perhaps should have "weathered the storm better, since they were essentially geared to the local economy" rather than being centres for State operation (Esmonde Cleary 1989, 153). However, since the rural farming economy had changed from simple subsistence to the necessary providing of surplus in order to comply with the taxation infrastructure of Roman government, and because the production of specialised crops and products had been encouraged by the local hierarchy, when things began to go badly for the Roman economy, the repercussions were wide-ranging, hard-felt, and fast in coming. The official withdrawal of Roman authority in 411 was the final straw; the disruption of the taxation cycle was "a blow the already weakened economy could not withstand" (*ibid*, 161). The landscape of Britain is littered with the archaeological evidence of towns in collapse, and it does not require the spectre of Saxon invaders to explain the devastation and abandonment present in most of these sites.

What happened after the official withdrawal of Roman authority from Britain is still a highly contentious area of academic discussion, but certainly, Dorchester remained a place where people settled, farmed, lived, worshipped and died, even as the landscape underwent changes both dramatic and subtle. Being 'Roman' in Dorchester slipped into the past and the inhabitants began the slow, often unconscious process of becoming something else.

Chapter Five

SHEDDING LIGHT ON "DARK AGE" DORCHESTER

"The conquering arms of our barbarian ancestors reached Civitas Durocina [Dorchester]. But what were the circumstances of this tragic conquest and destruction of a populous and wealthy city?" (Crake 1889)

As alluded to in the previous chapter, one may begin to see that, as Cleary suggests, Late Roman Britons were actually becoming something rather different from earlier Romano-Britons, and there is no reason to suspect that as the rot in the Empire spread out from the core, the systems of Roman order began to decay far earlier that 411 AD. With this decay of both governmental structure and ultimately, Christian contact, it is not difficult to imagine a return to customs long suppressed or altered. While late Roman Britain was ostensibly Christian, continuity at ancient sacred spaces, are indicators of lingering indigenous beliefs and indeed perhaps "they held beliefs not so very different from those of the newcomers from north-western Europe with whom they were to merge" (Henig 2007, 3). The Britons, in the absence of the power structure that had tacitly forced the hybridisation of their indigenous culture, may have been drawn to a return to their older pre-Christian, even pre-Roman customs. But with almost four centuries separating them from their ancestors, they may have been more willing than able to reclaim that past.

Dorchester burials

The one 'fact' most scholars are sure of when they write of early post-Roman Britain is that the Dorchester on Thames burials prove Anglo-Saxon troops were garrisoned at the towns. Like all 'facts', this too is ripe for deconstruction and alternatives. Whereas some seemingly immovable theories such as invasion and mass migration have finally been shifted, others, like the military implications of early Germanic evidence in Britain seem untouchable. While "few archaeologists today would argue that a burial containing Continental style dress ornaments was necessarily that of someone with immigrant forbears" (Hamerow 1999, 24), fewer might be comfortable with fourth century Germanic settlers, particularly outside of a military context. Yet that is precisely the suggestion made by Bartholomew when he argues that the 'Saxon Shore' is as likely to refer to a "shore settled by" the Saxons as it is a "shore attacked by" (1984, 185). He offers that since the only real evidence that exists for the latter is the assumption that the AD 367 crisis was sparked by Saxon invasions, but goes on to show how the real crisis was a food shortage that led to internal revolt and required the presence of Theodosius to resolve (*ibid*, 181). If this hypothesis can be considered, then it is likely that there were Saxons settling in Britain in the latter fourth century, at the time when everything was changing for the post-Roman Britons. A Germanic brooch in an early fifth century Abingdon burial (Everson and Knowles 1978, 125) exhibited evidence of much repair and was possibly a curated heirloom from a generation earlier, suggesting early presence in the region

During the previously mentioned wholesale destruction of the earthworks at Dyke Hills, two distinct burials were discovered and were after three-quarters of a century finally written up[13] (Kirk and Leeds

---

[13] Leeds received his information in 1914 from a local, Mr Cocks, who had been in 1870 an undergraduate observing, and lamenting, the destruction of the Dykes. There are many letters in the Dorchester Archive, Ashmolean Museum between Cocks, Rolleston, and MacFarlane debating the identification, preservation and provenance of the finds.

1954). Along with a third burial found north of the Minchin Recreation Ground (Figure 24) discovered some years later, the remains were interpreted as being Anglo-Saxon on the basis of their grave goods, although it has been argued that, based on the non-archaeological methods of excavation and preservation, we cannot say with any certainty that the male burial is in any way associated with the Germanic objects in the female burial, and indeed there is no evidence for the male being Anglo-Saxon at all (Esmonde Cleary 1989, 55-6). The reported artefacts included, for the women, continental brooches and for the man a peculiar form of ribbed belt (the bronze fittings remaining) and the suggestion of weapons.

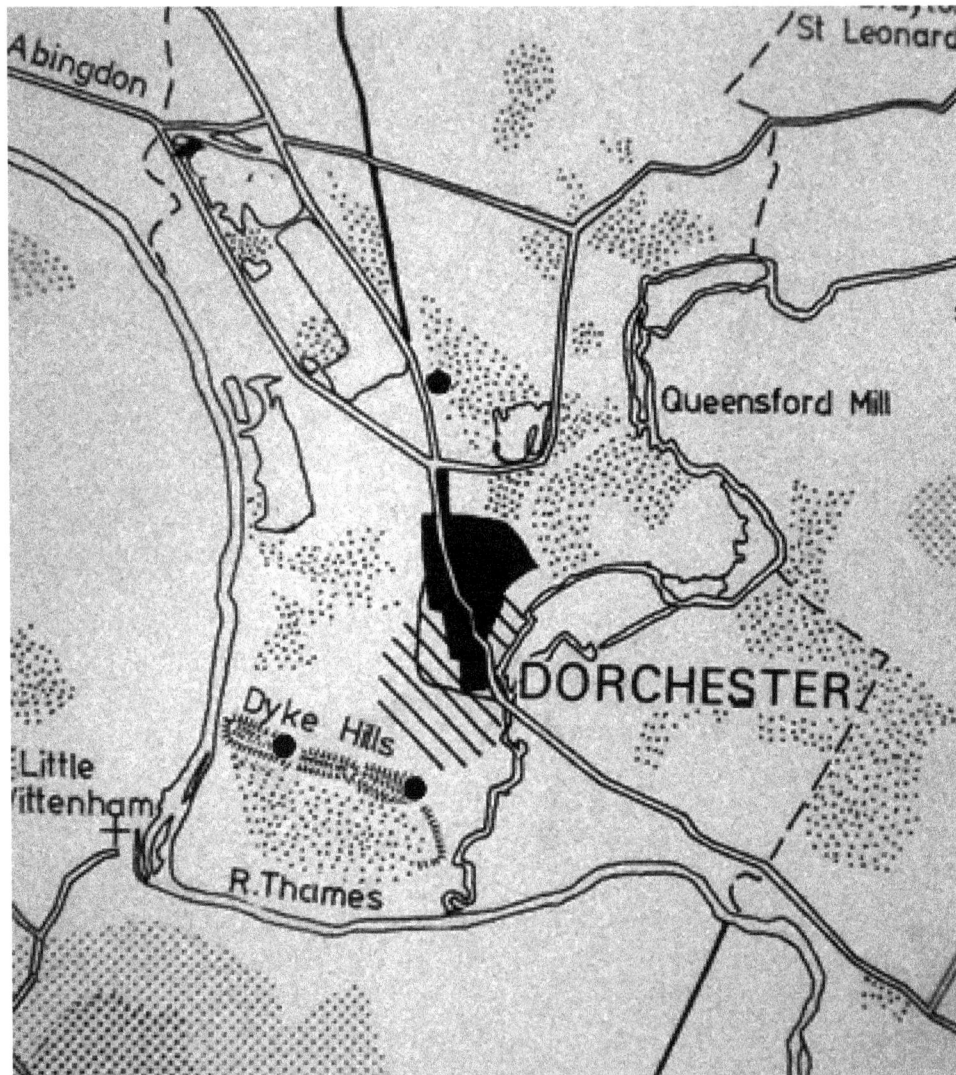

Figure 24. Findspots of the three main "Anglo Saxon" burials (after Munby and Rodwell 1974)

In truth, the 'weapons' are bits of iron that MacFarlane saw labourers throwing into the river, and it is uncertain if they were related to the burial, and a knife that, wrote Rolleston, "I should ascribe to the man" (*ibid*, 67), yet there is no contextual reason to do so. Offered as proof that the burial was of a soldier, a spear is occasionally attributed to the grave (Brooks 1986, 98), an error begun by a corpus (Swanton 1974, 43) that credits the Dyke Hills grave with a spear that actually was recovered from Atkinson's (1951) excavations north of the village, which revealed nine Saxon graves near a pre-historic barrow.

This single male representative of the Germanic presence in Dorchester has been offered as a mercenary, hired by the town of Dorchester to protect it after the withdrawal of Roman support, aided by an anomaly in coins concentrations that suggests the possible continuing payment of "troops to guard the Thames corridor" (Blair 1994, 186, ff 4). Yet the man's grave accessories are of a type not unusual from the continent in the late fourth century (Hawkes 1961, 6), and although the belt is unquestionably Roman military in nature, what proof do we have that this is not a veteran of continental service who has chosen to live out his days in the land where some of his Germanic kin were beginning to settle? Hawkes' claim "The presence of burials of such character on opposite sides of the town suggests that the Germanic military presence may have been larger than present evidence attests" (Hawkes 1986, 71) is a conclusion jumped to far too swiftly on too little evidence.

Hawkes makes the suggestion that the Minchin Recreation burial was a young Saxon woman who had made a curiosity collection of Roman artefacts: bronze key and rings, bracelets and male belt fittings. She argues that the objects "link her definitively with the military" yet without the precise information about how this burial was arranged, we have no real idea that this was a Saxon at all. The location of the burial, incorrectly identified for decades on distribution maps, was in fact some 200 metres to the north along a Roman road, not an unlikely place to find a Roman burial. Might this indicate a continuation of a Roman tradition? Surely it is possible that this woman was a 'Late Roman' Briton, sent to her grave with her 'chatelaine's' key and other personal possessions, and who had been given the imported brooches, which are rare even for the entire region.

As the Roman influence in daily life subsided, communities began living "a sub-Iron Age lifestyle, mixed oddly with half-forgotten Romanitas" (Blair 1994, 3). The Germanic settlers would not have been living in a completely alien manner; deprived (whether by force or choice) of much of their own culture for centuries, the Britons developed an affinity for objects of their continental neighbours. In exchange, the Britons influenced Germanic building styles and diverse structures much different from the continent were constructed (Dixon 1982, 279; Hamerow 1995, 16). Language too would have facilitated the transition. Based upon the isolation of Irish Celtic, we can see that prior to its heavy adulteration by Latin, the Celtic language possessed an almost Germanic phonetic structure (Schrijver 2008). These latent structures within the language, would have perhaps facilitated the ability to master the Germanic dialects of the new arrivals, and indeed there is some linguistic evidence for Celtic being the homogenising influence that gelled the various Frisian and Anglo-Saxon dialects into Old English (*ibid*) We know from genetic evidence that the scenario of Saxon mercenaries who got out of hand and wiped out the natives who hired them is unrealistic. A recent survey (Bodmer 2008) indicates that regional genetic makeup of the Oxfordshire region is a 51/49% split between ancient British and Anglo-Saxon descent. Moreover, the chaotic state of affairs in late fourth century and early fifth century Britain may have created an atmosphere of uncertainty into which new settlers and abandoned Britons found themselves together trying to form order from the chaos that was generated by the vacuum of the Roman administrative and economic withdrawal and collapse.

Urban Sunken Featured Buildings

Discussion of Dorchester's continuity of 'urban' life often has as its centre the presence of an early Saxon SFB, or *grubenhaus*, excavated in the allotments by Frere in 1962. This SFB appears to respect the Roman metalled streets (Figure 25) and suggests that the town layout was at least visible and possibly in use when the Saxon hut was cut into the Roman layers.

The occupation evidence for this building was very small; only a few Saxon sherds were found, which Frere dated to just prior to AD550. This date should be viewed with some caution however, as such sherds as were found were "lacking major diagnostic features" (*ibid, 149)*. Frere argued his date by comparing his plain sherds with some Cassington plain sherds that were found in association with a failed brooch casting; by dating the brooch style, he arrived at a date for the Dorchester sherds. While this might be correct, the unremarkable nature of the scant sherds from the SFB make it necessary to try to get better dating from this area, or at least a new diagnostic for the sherds.

This SFB is rather unusual in that, for a supposedly primitive structure, it possessed a vestibule (Frere 162, 123) and steps that led down into the main interior from the street. Although there was some indication of stakeholes that may have supported floorboards, the successive re-floorings of yellow loam, suggest that there was not a suspended floor as is argued for many SFBs in other areas. The strange nature of the feature allowed for the creation of a very unique-looking reconstruction (Figure 26). It is of course uncertain if this bears any resemblance to the actual structure.

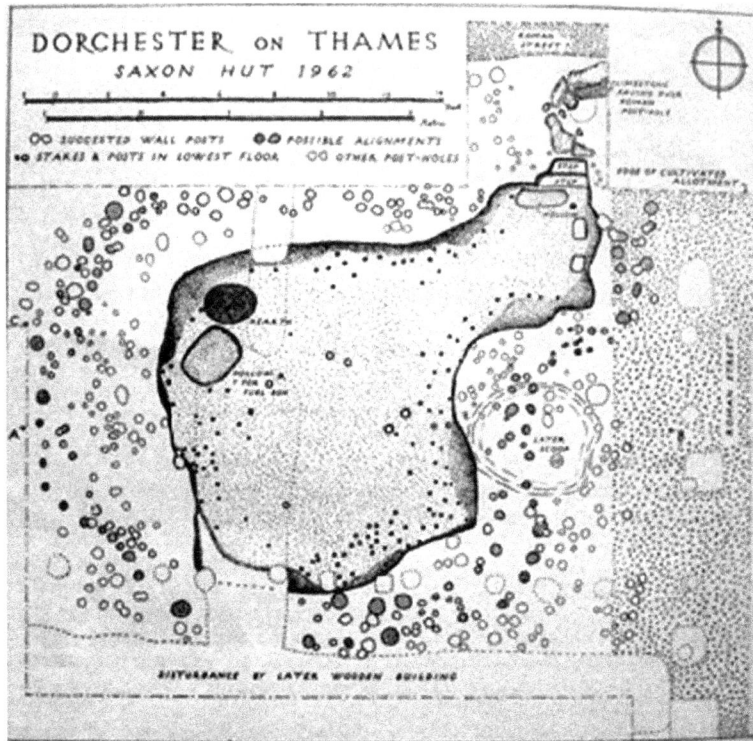

Figure 25. Detail of the Dorchester Allotment SFB (Frere 1962)

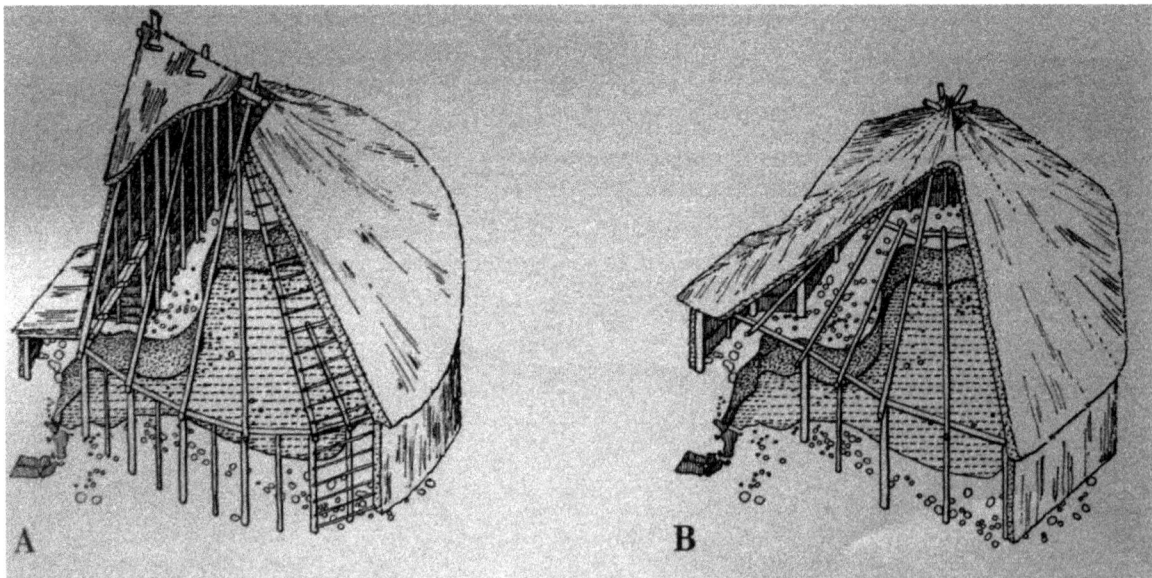

Figure 26. Two possible reconstructions of the Dorchester Allotment SFB (Frere 1962)

Frere believed that, based upon the proximity to the Late Roman stone footed building that had been constructed over the coin if Honorius, it was likely that the SFB represented the native habits of Germanic soldiers garrisoned on the town, in the traditional model of poet-Roman Britain, which called for British tyrants hiring mercenaries. The SFB contained a hearth and two possible ovens, so it is possible it was used for cooking only, and served as an auxiliary building. Yet it is impossible to make a military link between the SFB and the Late Roman building, since at the very least, a century could separate their use. Subsequent excavations have revealed an SFB near the Abbey (Keevil 2003), and two at Beech House Hotel (Rowley and Brown 1981); Castle Inn (Bradley 1978) might have had two as well, although the excavator was hesitant to press the claim (R Bradley, *pers comm*). Dating evidence was in these instances rather scant, but a sixth century date is likely, with the Abbey site providing what has been tentatively offered as a rare early green- glazed pottery of Byzantine origin (Keevil 2003, 343)

That there was "cultural mingling" (Brooks 1988, 99) between the Britons and the Saxons has been stated above, and the evidence presented, in addition to the presence of late cemeteries around Dorchester that exhibit both British and Saxon traditions indicate a degree of co-habitation. What becomes implausible is the argument that some cultural intermingling went on within structured towns and created an overlap of urban life and function into the early medieval period. Clearly, there was some continued activity within the physical limits of the town at Dorchester, but after the radical changes of the late fourth century, Dorchester was likely not functioning in any way that could sustain a continued urban existence. What remained in the town by the fifth century, subject to ruin and decay, was likely made use of on occasion and in a manner in keeping with the new demands of the local lifestyle and cultural choices.

One should not imply the value judgment that civilised life came to an end and people lived dark, miserable lives in their grubby little hut. Blair likens these people to "children stumbling across a demolition site and picking up fragments of debris… [taking] the structures left by the Iron Age and Roman communities and us[ing] them in their own more primitive ways" (1998, xxv). This is an unfair assessment. They made culturally appropriate choices that did not involve carrying on a Romanised standard of life. An example might be the fate of Victoria Station in Mumbai, India. At the height of the British Empire, it was an impressive piece of British architecture, dominating the Bombay landscape. Now, although still an efficient, functioning rail station, the once gloriously tiled floors are chipped away in places to accommodate other needs, animals are frequent, and the front entrance is partially used to store a large pile of soil. To Western eyes, it might look shabby, in bad repair, and dirty. Yet the community has made a conscious choice to adapt the western building to function in a manner suited to them. There is nothing shabby or primitive about it, and neither would there have been when fifth and sixth century families chipped through mosaic floors to build their ovens.

Princely town

In the first part of the seventh century, Dorchester became an ecclesiastical centre, due to the selection of the location by Birinus, an Italian bishop sent to England to facilitate the spread of Christianity. He established his church in 635 and for nearly 30 years, Dorchester remained see of Wessex, until threats from Mercian activity necessitated a move to Winchester (Munby and Rodwell 1974, 103). In 1974, Dickinson, based on little more than an assumption of continuity and a few antiquarian stray finds, advanced an argument that Dorchester was a princely settlement. As the "archaeological evidence for the existence there of a very rich settlement" (25), she offered three gold coins listed rather imprecisely by antiquarians as being found "somewhere in Dorchester", which referred to the entire Dorchester Hundred. Although one *solidus* was dated 364-375, based on the popularity of mounting such coins for pendants in the early medieval period, she attributed all to the early seventh century. Added to these coins was a 1776 find of a pyramidal gold stud (Figure 27), elaborately decorated with cloisonné and set garnets (Dickinson 1974, 28). Dickinson drew connections with Sutton Hoo craftsmanship, and claimed the stud likely came from that workshop and belonged to a man of great wealth and importance, with a jeweller on staff. From this she extrapolated the presence of a "princely burial" in Dorchester, similar to one at Cuddesdon, and argued that Birinus and the see of Wessex would have been drawn by the presence of this influential man, as the power base of the area. Biddle had advanced a similar argument, that Dorchester was a "place of royal importance that had emerged from late Roman Britain" (1971, 396). It surely seems a heavy burden for one tiny gold stud to bear. A more plausible hypothesis might be, given the ambiguous dating of these stray finds, after the installation of a Bishop at Dorchester, powerful men who wished to increase their prestige by showing their connection to the Church would have travelled to Dorchester, where the stud may have been lost.

Figure 27. Sketch of the cloisonné gold stud taken from the Society of Antiquaries of London 1776 Minute Book. It is the only trace remaining of this object and regrettably, the drawing was done with such skill as might prove terribly useful. (after Dickinson 1974, 54)

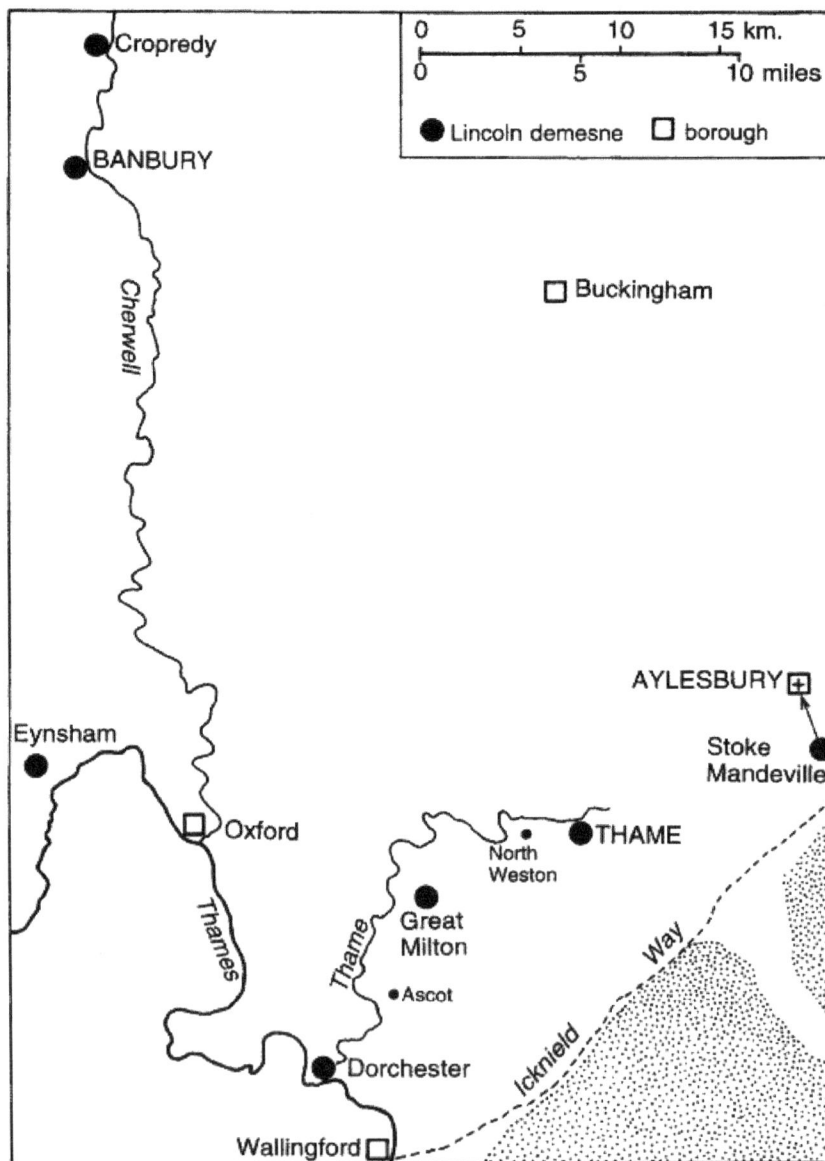

Figure 28. The major estates of the eleventh century see of Dorchester-on-Thames in the Upper Thames Valley (after Blair 2001, 118)

Why Birinus chose Dorchester is a matter of some debate. Bede tells us that Birinus baptised the king Cynegils at Dorchester, in the presence of the Northumbrian king Oswald, an event that led to a marriage connecting the two kingdoms and to the Upper Thames Valley falling heavily under the political dominance of Northumbria (Blair 1994, 44). What we are not told, however is what brought two of the most powerful men on the island to Dorchester specifically. It may have been, as suggested in a previous chapter, that the fusion of pagan and Christian beliefs and rituals had preserved some aspects of Christianity in the region, which Birinus would have hoped to build upon. Some scholars believe that the preservation of Christianity in southern Britain was likely in small pockets (Henig and Booth 2000, 185), whilst others seem certain that this is little more than wishful thinking unsupported by any real evidence (1994,3). Perhaps the religion of the inhabitants around the defunct Roman town was not the issue at all, but rather the ancestral tradition of linking Dorchester and its environs with the liminal realm of spirituality and ritual. Or perhaps the role that Dorchester had played in the Roman world was significant enough in local memory to warrant that new representative of Rome, the church, to set up operations in that location. The attempted adoption of *romanitas* was often part of justifying the assumption of power and authority during this period.

Later, Cynegils heir Cenwealh would offend the great pagan king of Mercia, Penda and found himself in exile from his kingdom when Birinus died. It was some time before a new bishop was appointed in the form of Agilbert, a Frank. Cenwealh reportedly longed for a bishop who spoke his own tongue, so he split the province into tow sees, and established Bishop Wine at Winchester. Naturally, Agilbert took umbrage at this usurpation of his position and returned to the continent. The newly made bishop of Winchester also ran afoul of Cenwealh not long after and the entire province was without a bishop for a while. When a replacement was found, he was installed at Winchester. Dorchester had lost its chance for political greatness, it seemed. Indeed, one scholar has claimed that were it not for Penda, Dorchester "might have become the capital if united England" (Blair 1994, 45).

Ninth century Viking incursions in other more vulnerable parts of the country forced the re-instating of the bishopric at Dorchester around 870, and this suggests that there may have been, in the interim absence, a continued religious community in the village. Indeed, archaeological excavation has revealed seventh to ninth century rectangular halls not unlike domestic structures found at other religious sites. However, whatever secular importance the region once held had so drastically diminished that by the late Saxon period, Dorchester was passed over in favour of other locations such as nearby Wallingford and Oxford.

Of Birinus' church, nothing remains, but there is no reason to suppose that the subsequent churches did not rest on the same spot. The history of the current building can be in part read by looking at its architecture. There is some speculation that the eleventh century church, possibly built by Remegius of Winchester, is still partly extant in the Norman structure that now stands. The holdings of the Dorchester bishopric were vast and would have generated a great deal if income for the church (Figure 28), but it is obvious that little of this wealth was invested back into the Dorchester Hundred. By 1072 the see was removed for the last time to Lincoln and in 1140 the former cathedral was used by a chapter of Augustinian canons. Birinus, now sainted, had been buried in Winchester, but in 1225 some of is purported relics were returned to Dorchester and his tomb became a focus for pilgrimage. This must have been beneficial to the town as well as the church, and over the next century money was raised for the expansion of the church from a simple cruciform plan to the construction of choir aisles to the north and south, as well as a bell tower. At the dissolution of the monasteries, the church holdings were turned to parochial use, the medieval records destroyed. Dorchester became a place on the road to and from Oxford and although for a time a thriving coaching economy sprung up in the seventeenth and eighteenth centuries, spawning no less than ten inns at its zenith, the village quietly stepped from the national historic stage.

The Abbey at Dorchester has generated much interest and attention, not the least of which has been for its incredible aesthetic appeal. The history and archaeology of the Abbey has been well served by Rodwell's recent, though as yet unpublished, three-volume monograph. Several books have been written about its unique contributions to the discussion of church architecture, and the features of note, such as the Jesse Window (Figure 29), the brass grave plaques and reclining knight effigy (Figure 30) are well known.

Figure 29.Detail of the Jesse Window (l); interior of Dorchester Abbey (Abbey church of St Peter and St Paul). (images courtesy Howard Stanbury (l), Pam Brophy(r))

Figure 30. Effigy on a tomb in Dorchester Abbey, peculiar for its twisted body and frozen sword-drawing action. Listed by Skeleton in the 19th century as "The tomb of the unknown knight", it is widely regarded as the tomb of Robert of Little Holcombe, a documented land holder in 1241. (Photograph by Thomas Photos, courtesy Oxfordshire County Council Photographic Archive)

A theological college for missionary students was established at the former monastic rectory in 1878, largely through the exertions of the antiquarian vicar, W. C. Macfarlane. Its purpose was to train clergymen for missionary work in the colonies. However, the Great War drastically reduced the numbers of men available for such exercises, and by the middle of the Second World War, the college was closed. The Bodleian Archive in Oxford maintains a collection of newsletters that used to be published by the missionary college; from this tiny village, missionaries spanned the globe and wrote back to share their adventures with the Oxfordshire community. The blatant imperial tone and 'political incorrectness' of the age are almost offensive in some cases, but they preserve the worldview of the era and are part of the Dorchester history. Today that building houses the Dorchester Abbey museum, filled with displays that highlight Dorchester's significant contributions to the history mankind's activity in the region for the past several millennia.

Chapter Six

TWO TALES OF A CITY?

"Each generation of scholars has imposed its own views and prejudices on the evidence in an attempt to explain the inanimate scraps..."   (Cunliffe 2005)

In the beginning of the research process that led to this book, it was believed that a rather straightforward, but more detailed history of Dorchester would be related. The story has been told over and over with such increasing distillation that Dorchester has often been summed up in a few simple sentences. It was hoped that the Dorchester story could be re-invigorated by the inclusion of recent details and that its place in the broader context of southern Britain would be clearer. However, along the way, an interesting thing occurred. Alternative hypotheses crept into the narrative, which allowed for a different story to emerge for Dorchester, one not entirely in keeping with the orthodoxy but with the potential to make us rethink what we were certain we already knew. What follows is the presentation of those two differing histories based on the evidence of the prior chapters.

Scenario One

The traditional story of Dorchester is well known; it begins in the Neolithic with the creation of a ritual complex of monuments and funerary features that appear to have some cosmological alignment. Later Bronze Age funerary monuments were constructed in this region along side the older features. A late Bronze Age/ Early Iron Age settlement across the river at Castle Hill was the focus of the area, providing both refuge and a place for aggregation. By the Middle Iron Age, Castle Hill had been abandoned, as communities gave up hillforts for valley settlement. Nearby Mount Farm was a typical Iron Age homestead, but the proto-urban *oppidum* at Dyke Hills was the power centre for the area at the end of the Late Iron Age, until AD 43.

After the conquest, a fort was established to protect Roman interests on the road between Alcester and Silchester. A vicus that grew up around the fort eventually merged into the growing town, which was enclosed by ramparts in the second century, and by stone walls in the third. An administrative centre, as evidenced by the presence of a *beneficiarius consularis*, Dorchester remained an important place, even after the decline of the Empire in Britain, as foederati were employed to protect the town from the ensuing chaos of the fifth century. Continuing to reside in the Roman town, and perhaps even attempting to carry on with some form of Roman life, Britons and Saxons lived side by side, until the dominant Saxon culture overtook them. A powerful leader emerged in the late sixth, early seventh century whose wealth and influence may have persuaded Birinus to establish his church at Dorchester in AD635.

Scenario Two

In 1983, Richard Reece wrote a book called *My Roman Britain*; while not so bold as to assign the subtitle "My Dorchester-on-Thames", I offer this second scenario as an alternative synthesis of the evidence.

What began as a series of funerary monuments, perhaps inspired by the meeting place of two powerful rivers, was later incorporated into a great cursus; the Neolithic ritual complex at Dorchester influenced the later placement of Bronze Age funerary monuments and the significance of journeying to the region for sacred activity may have added to the attractiveness of the area for settlement. Bronze Age farmers laid out the land in ditched field systems and by the Late Bronze Age had settled the top of the most visible landmark in the area, Castle Hill. A hill fort was constructed there sometime during the Bronze Age/ Iron Age transition, but socio-economic changes of the Middle Iron Age led people to seek alternatives in their settlement patterns. Perhaps as early as this, a settlement grew up along the banks on the opposite side of the river. Earthworks were constructed, either for defence or in a conspicuous display of labour resources. The position of this settlement near the two rivers may have lent it a sacred aspect, and it is equally likely that it was a centre for trading, sited at a nexus between two major waterways and trackways that had been in long use. Imports from as far away as the Mediterranean made their way to the Dorchester.

As economic links between the Roman continent and Britain strengthened, Dorchester continued its role as a place of trade and congregation. Roman traders established a small community and the Britons grew more and more accustomed to their ways, and provided no real resistance to the events of AD 43. Not part of a fort, the timber buildings thrown up were not military in nature but rather the sort of building one would expect a continental trader to build if he were going to live among his consumers. Following the upheaval of the 60's, the town was completely razed to impose a more orderly format to the town, perhaps with an influx of continental inhabitants to preclude any further insurrections.

One of the ways for Romano-British elites to assert their wealth, power, influence or loyalties in the town environment was to practice munificence, that is, the construction of baths, temples, or other notable structures at their expense and ostensibly for the good of the town. Yet Dorchester is seemingly devoid of such features. Could this imply that there was an alternative mechanism for exhibiting one's standing within the town? What might that mechanism be and can we detect anything from the archaeological record? Perhaps the abundance of scattered coinage, possibly indicative of prolific hoard deposition, suggests that the town's importance was less as a "variant of the normal economically functioning town" (Millett 1995, 36), but rather as a continuing location for religious activity. Millett quite rightly suggests that our modern secularisation of life causes us to project a similar view backward, neglecting the role that ritual and religious practice would have had on every aspect of life, including the growth and development of towns.

The construction of the town walls, if not for civic defence could have been erected as an indication of status. Formal approval needed to be granted by the Emperor, thus the very act of laying a wall indicated his favour. The wall would also serve to channel travel through the town and help in the collection of taxation and duties upon transport, although, as Esmonde Cleary writes (2003, 83), "control of ingress and egress took second place to display". The wall would not only have created an impressive entry into the town, but would also have marked the sacred 'town' space from the profane 'outside'. Perhaps the secret to Dorchester's enduring significance lies in the cumulative effect of millennia of sacred activity taking place at a geographically well-suited location, being easily accessed both by prehistoric trackways and by the rivers.

The traditional quest for continuity hopes to identify a continued occupation often neglecting the fact the continuity really desired is a "continuity of traditional socio-economic and institutional patterns along Roman or quasi-Roman lines" (Burnham1995, 14). Rowley suggests a different term is needed, and that "whatever else happened, Romano-British Dorchester did not survive in to the sixth century" (1974, 48). Indeed, there was little Roman left about the Late Romano-Britons; we should refer to them as post-Roman Britons (Esmonde Cleary 1989) whose lifestyles and culture had moved on after the decay and collapse of Roman influence, even before the official withdrawal.

With the major changes at the end of the Roman period, Dorchester's inhabitants began to revert to a more traditional, rustic way of life that in some ways may have resembled pre-Roman culture, but had too many foreign elements now bound up in it. Neither flesh nor fowl nor good red herring, the inhabitants were open to influences that spoke to their societal needs and cultural tastes on a comprehensible level. Germanic styles from the continent were not so far removed as to have seemed alien, and were readily adopted by a population looking for something to latch onto and make their own.

Rome was in the past, and there was no point looking back, yet the Dorchester area was still compelling, perhaps not only for its arable land and water resources. Perhaps one should consider the continuing significance of Dorchester in the post Roman period prior to the arrival of Birinus as being similar to its significance in the Neolithic. We have no good settlement evidence, no indication that people in the Neolithic felt the need to actually *live* in the area simply in order to be connected with it on a deeper level. Just so, there is no need to argue for a continuity of life in the old Roman town, when the significance of the locality as a marker of personal identity is sufficient enough to explain its longevity of influence. There may have been only scattered habitation in the area, with few if any people actually dwelling within the decayed remains of the walled town, but the numbers buried in the surrounding late cemeteries testify to the presence of nearby inhabitants. The place-memory associations of the town proper, along with the possible amalgamation of lingering Christian beliefs and older native traditions, may have marked the place for notice when Birinus came to England.

Thus at Dorchester, perhaps we do after all have continuity, but it is not the continuity of Roman life that Frere and others read into the scraps of evidence from the post-Roman period. The idea of a pocket of Romanised (whatever that is!) inhabitants trying to hold on to town functions and culture, a last bastion until the "new Rome" in the guise of the Church arrived to re-establish order, must be seen to be fantastic. The continuity rather is nothing so grand, and yet perhaps is the grandest of all: a continuity of endurance, of human survival and persistence. Not the submission of the population to the swords and spears of invaders, but unrelenting adaptation to the "slings and arrows of outrageous fortune".

Chapter Seven

EPILOGUE – WHAT LIES AHEAD?

"There is a lot more to learn about Dorchester but I can say I am only interested in the earlier part!"
(S S Frere, pers comm)

The story of Dorchester-on-Thames and its fascinating role in the story of human habitation of the Thames valley reveals itself, like any complex and special place, as a series of narratives. This dissertation has attempted to outline two of those narratives, which are inextricably intertwined: the narrative of human occupation of the location and the narrative of discovery by antiquarian and archaeologists over the past several centuries. The first storyline is made possible by the efforts of those whose actions are detailed in the second. Like the fine work placed on a growing tapestry, the extent of our knowledge, our image of ancient Dorchester becomes increasingly more rich and clear, with every plunge and surge of the needle, or in this analogy, the excavator's trowel. Yet in spite of the wealth of information we currently possess from Dorchester, there remains so much that is unknown. The tapestry is only partly completed, and the images are still clouded by the gaps in our knowledge. Dorchester has been at the very heart of the story of British archaeology. Here was found the inspiration and motivation for preserving our ancient monuments with acts of legislation, thanks in part to General Pitt-Rivers. Here too were Allen and Crawford's fledgling days of aerial photography experienced. Some of the first modern "salvage" archaeology took place at the Big Rings under Atkinson during the Second World War and one of the first applications of resistivity geophysical survey was undertaken at that time during that excavation (Clark 1997, 12-15). Yet there is so much more to know and to do. How many other great firsts in archaeology might Dorchester be a part of? Only further survey and excavation can render a more complete understanding, for there are areas of Dorchester which both study and intuition indicate are of vast significance to Dorchester's past, yet which have remained unexplored. The following pages will outline what may be the more important research goals for any future work in Dorchester.

Neolithic cursus

Nearly all of Dorchester's cursus has been obliterated by gravel extraction and the by-pass construction, and in 1988 it was reported that only the north-west terminal should be extant, although its position was unknown (Bradley and Chambers, 275) However, aerial photography seems to reveal a 30m length of cursus remnant within a small triangular portion of land just southwest of the bypass and directly north of the Minchin Recreation Ground and adjacent lake. This field also seems to contain two small circular ditches. What more could these fragmentary remains tell us beyond what is already known of the cursus? Most importantly they are the last pristine vestiges of a lost monument. They should be preserved and any excavation carried out on them severely restricted without clear research objectives. However, if there is doubt about the dating of the cursus, or if the ring ditches would help us to better understand the nature of the monuments at Dorchester, then this small patch of land represents the last hope for modern examination of the Neolithic feature, without being under duress of development.

Dyke Hills

Obviously, the area of greatest potential, not only for Dorchester, but also for any study of the Iron Age Thames Valley region is that of the earthworks at Dyke Hills and its enclosed space. Fundamentally, and least invasively, there is an urgent need to conduct geophysical surveys of the assumed *oppidum*, in order to complement our aerial photographic record of crop marks. Also, a simple regime of augering for soil and environmental analysis, whilst not seriously impacting the integrity of the land, might produce a more comprehensive picture of the river levels over time (Figure 31) Additionally, conservation efforts of the standing earthworks must be re-doubled, as the ravages of rampant rabbit activity are rapidly laying waste to the monument, as well as disturbing what may be significant stratigraphic relationships as they work artefacts and soils to the top through warren construction.

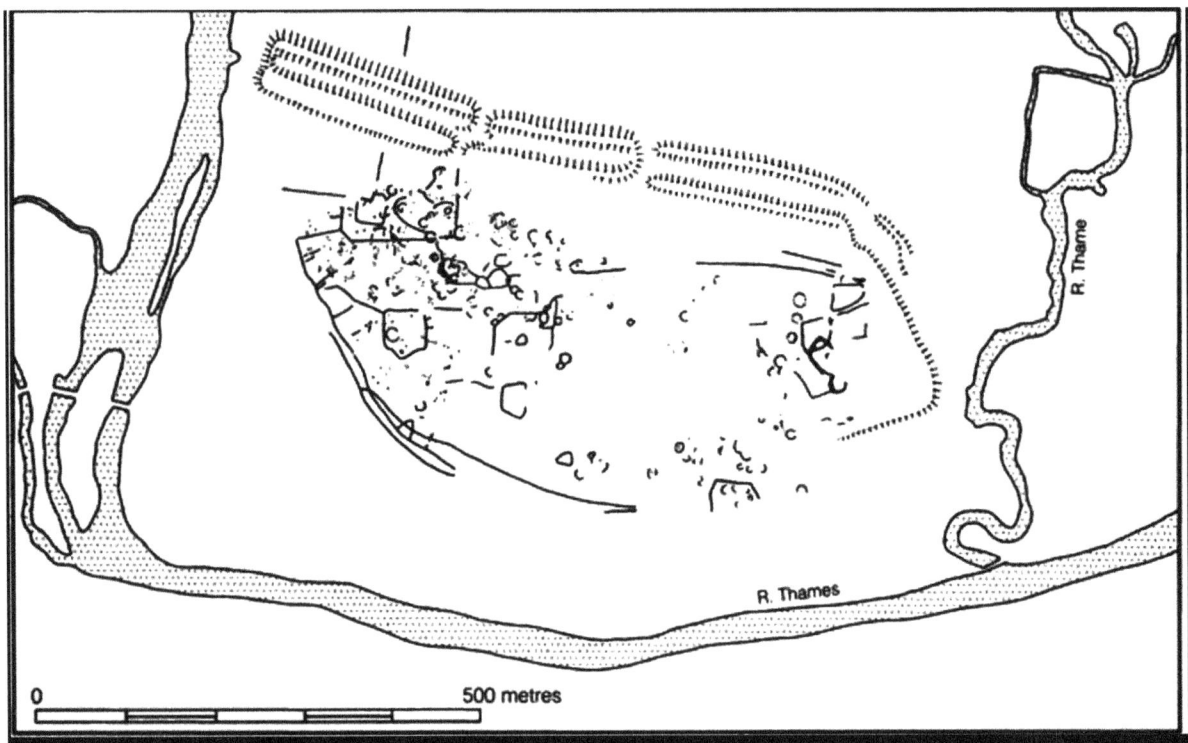

Figure 31. Interior of Dyke Hills enclosure with major cropmarks drawn, highlighting the importance of resolving the Iron Age location of the riverfront by the obvious blank area on the approach to the present day riverside. (after Cunliffe 2005, 403)

Ideally, following sensitive communications that stress a sympathetic understanding of the needs of agriculture balanced with the needs of archaeology, there would be a change of heart from the recalcitrant landowner and small-scale excavation would be permitted with in the '*oppidum*', in order to establish a firm dating sequence of occupation there, with an emphasis on riverside activity, in order to begin to define the role of the settlement and its relationship to the Thames. A small intervention across the earthwork might also remove the last traces of doubt concerning the identity of the monument's constructors.

Of course with regard to the Dyke Hills, there is also some work that could be done with artefacts already in possession of the museums. The human remains from the two individuals currently housed with the Oxfordshire County Museum Service at Standlake should be radiocarbon dated in order to establish if they are contemporary with the more famous burials that reside in the British Museum. Those remains too, would benefit from modern examination, and although there is still much room for scrutiny in the results of isotopic analysis, such examination of these assumedly Germanic remains should be carried out.

Dorchester allotments

One of the most severe limitations upon Frere's excavations in the heart of the Roman town was the cultivation of the various allotments. This necessitated an excavation strategy that maximised the exploration of the area while respecting the horticultural and agricultural labours of the village residents. Unfortunately, this restricted view of the Roman town beneath the fertile soil inhibited a full interpretation of the archaeology and much was left to assumption (Figure 18). A future excavation should seek to resolve not only the questions that were remaining in Frere's mind at the end of his work there, but also to create a more inclusive plan of the settlement.

One area of Frere's excavation that most requires re-visiting is that of the early Saxon *grubenhaus* in the north of the allotments. The techniques now available to us may be able to more precisely indicate the date of this feature and its place in the story of decline or continuity at Dorchester. Curiously no other SFBs were located in the allotments, Rowley's SFBs were of a peculiar nature, and Bradley only tentatively allowed that one feature could be a possible *grubenhaus*. Solitary SFBs are known, but surely locating more of them would strengthen the 'continuity of town life' thesis. The physical limitations of Frere's allotment excavation may have created this apparent lack of features; therefore it is imperative to open up a larger portion of the northern end of the area in order to establish the relationship Frere's SFB may have had with other contemporary features. Additionally, there were two large post-Roman ditches, one of which showed evidence of postholes (Frere 1984, 119). Frere was unable to excavate enough area to determine if they were fences or served another purpose. In recent discussion with him, he was still curious about these ditches and they should be examined in more detail.

Another area of work that should be explored is the pottery assemblage from the 1962-3 excavations. Housed at the Ashmolean museum, this assemblage of sherds is long overdue for a re-evaluation, regrettably one whose scale lay outside the scope of this thesis. Of particular interest would be the sherds that are listed in the report as Saxon, followed by the caveat (Romano-British?). If accurate placement of these sherds within a ceramic chronology for Oxfordshire can be done, then there will be more secure factual data to bring to the urban continuity/ early Saxon settlement discussion.

The area of mettalling briefly described by Hassall (Wilson 1965, 210) extending, 33.5m x 35m over the top of some first century timber buildings should be examined further. This large area, too large to be merely a road, may have served as a forum or market place. Serious consideration of explorations into areas adjacent to this former orchard should be taken. This would require the cooperation and enthusiastic participation of the local community, to allow either test pitting or geophysical survey to be conducted in their back gardens, but approached sensitively, some percentage of the inhabitants would be likely to be accommodating.

Dorchester's early Roman period

The nature of the first century Roman settlement is crucial in understanding the growth and development of the town. In addition to resolving the question of the existence of a fort, better knowledge of this period would also shed some light upon the relationship between the native occupants of the region and the growing Roman settlement. The traces of first century timber buildings, revealed in part by Frere's work lying under the southern ramparts and under the stone building in the centre of the allotments, as well as by Hassall in the orchards north of the allotments, require further attention as they could reveal more information about the nature of the open settlement that existed prior to the supposed fort, and certainly prior to the first wave of defensive constructions.

Dorchester's defences

Although the arguments have been made above about the importance of understanding the location of the defences, it is also a research priority to accurately date them. As detailed above, the rampart and ditched defences have had approximate dates given and refuted for the past three-quarters of a century. Even the most current monograph to discuss Dorchester couches the rampart dating in such careful terms as "presumably" and "probably" (Booth *et al* 2007, 74). That this uncertainty should continue in this modern era of advanced dating techniques is an embarrassment, and one that could quite easily be remedied.

As to the areas considered by many to be outside the defences, of the eastern side of the village, little is known. However, thanks to the kind cooperation of the landowners, the Vicarage Garden, from whence the elaborate cremation burial emerged in the nineteenth century, will be examined with geophysical survey and a test pit, along with a few other locations nearby. These small peeks into the eastern extremity of the Roman town may deliver a large return on so small an investment of time and labour; they may reveal nothing new. But regardless of the result, they will add to the long history of archaeological enquiry and boundless local enthusiasm for the story of human settlement and activity in this place of enduring significance.

REFERENCES

Aitchison, N B, 1988 "Hoards and Hoarding", *World Arch* **20 (2)**, 270-84

Alföldy, G, 1974 (trans T Birley) *Noricum*, London: Routledge and Kegan Paul

Allen, T G, 2000 "The Iron Age background", in Henig and Booth 2000, 1-33

Atkinson R J C, **Piggott**, C M, and **Sandars**, N K, 1951 *Excavations at Dorchester, Oxon*, Oxford: Ashmolean Museum

Barclay, A, **Cromarty**, A M, **Lambrick**, G, and **Robinson**, M, 2005 "Synthesis: the wider regional and national context" in (eds A M   Cromarty, G Lambrick, A Barclay, and M Robinson) "*Late Bronze Age Ritual and Habitation on a Thames Eyot at Whitecross Farm, Wallingford*, Oxford: Oxford Archaeology, 225-36

Barclay, A, and **Hey**, G, 1999 "Cattle, cursus monuments and the river: the development of ritual and domestic landscapes in the Upper Thames Valley, in (eds A Barclay and J Harding) *Pathways and ceremonies: the cursus monuments of Britain and Ireland*, Oxford: Oxbow, 67-76

Barclay, A J, **Lambrick**, G, **Moore**, J, and **Robinson**, M 2003 Lines *in the Landscape, Cursus Monuments in the Upper Thames Valley: Excavations at the Drayton and Lechlade   cursuses,* Oxford: Oxford Archaeology

Barker, G, 2006 *The Agricultural Revolution: Why Did Foragers Become Farmers*, Oxford: University Press

Bartholomew, P, 1984 "Fourth-century Saxons", *Britannia* **15**, 169-185

Bartlett, R, 1988 "The Harlow Celtic temple: a Celtic shrine underlies the famous Roman temple" *Current Archaeology* **112**, 162-66

Behrens, G, 1954, "Romische Kult-Gefäβe", *Germania* **30**, 111-12,

Benson, D, and **Miles**, D, 1974 *The Upper Thames Valley: An Archaeological Survey of the River Gravels*, Oxford: Oxford Archaeology

Biddle, M, 1971 "Archaeology and the beginnings of English society", in (eds P Clemoes and K Hughes) *England before the Conquest: studies in primary sources presented to Dorothy Whitelock*, Cambridge: University Press, 391-408

Bertram, C, 1809 *The description of Britain,* London: Richard Taylor and Company

Blair, J, 1994 *Anglo Saxon Oxfordshire* Stroud: Sutton

Blair, J, 2001 "Estate Memoranda of C. 1070 from the See of Dorchester-on-Thames", *The English Historical Review* **116**, 114-23

Bodmer, W, 2008 "The genetic structure of the British population", a lecture given at the Europa day conference, May 17, 2008: Oxford

Booth, P, **Dodd**, A, **Robinson**, M, and **Smith**, A, 2007 *The Thames through time-the archaeology of the gravel terraces of the Upper and Middle Thames:the early historical period: AD 1-1000*, Oxford: Oxford Archaeology

Bradford, J S P, 1942 "An Early Iron Age site at Allen's Pit, Dorchester", *Oxon* **7**, 28-42

Bradford, J S P, and **Goodchild**, R G, 1939 "Excavations at Frilford, Berks, 1937-8",*Oxon* **4**, 1-80

Bradley, R, 1978 "Rescue Excavation at Dorchester-on-Thames", *Oxon* **43**, 17-39

Bradley, R, 1986 "The Bronze Age in the Oxford area- its local and regional significance", in (eds G Biggs, J Cook, and T Rowley) *The archaeology of the Oxford region*, Oxford: University Department for External Studies, 39-48

Bradley, R, 1992 "The gravels and British prehistory from the Neolithic to the early Iron Age", in (eds M Fulford and E Nichols) *Developing landscapes of lowland Britain: the archaeology of   the British gravels*, London: Society of Antiquaries,15-22

Bradley, R, and **Chambers**, R A, 1988 "A new study of the cursus complex at Dorchester on Thames", *Oxon* **7**(3), 271-89

Bradley, R, and **Smith**, A C, 2007 "Questions of context: a Greek cup from the River Thames", in (eds C Gosden, H Hamerow, P DeJersey and G Lock) *Communities and connections: essays   in honour of Barry Cunliffe*, 30-42

Bradley, R, and **Yates**, D, 2007 "After 'Celtic' fields: the social organisation of Iron Age agriculture" in (eds C Haselgrove and R Pope) *The earlier Iron Age in Britain and the near continent*, Oxford: Oxbow, 94-102

Brooks, J A, 1986 "Continuity in British towns in the fifth and sixth centuries", *Oxford J Archaeol* **5**, 77-102

Brooks, J A, 1988 "The case for continuity in fifth-century Canterbury re-examined", *Oxon* **7**, 99-114

Burnham, B C, 1986 "The origins of Romano-British small towns",*Oxford J Arch* **5** (2), 185-203

Burnham, B C, 1988 "The morphology of Romano-British small towns", *Archaeol J* **144**, 156-190

Burnham, B C, 1995 "Small towns; the British perspective", in (ed A E Brown) *Roman small towns in eastern England and beyond*, Oxford: Oxbow, 7-15

Burnham, B C, and **Wacher**, J S, 1990 *The small towns of Roman Britain*, London: B T Batsford

Case, H, 1986 "The Mesolithic and Neolithic in the Oxford region", in (eds G Biggs, J Cook, and T Rowley) *The archaeology of the Oxford region*, Oxford: University Department for External Studies,18-37

Chambers, R A,1982 "An excavation across the northern defences of the Roman town at Dorchester on Thames, Oxon 1981", Oxford   Archaeology report (unpublished)

Chambers, R A, 1984 "Dorchester, 51 ", *Oxford Arch Newsletter,* **9(1)**

Chambers, R A, 1986 *Archaeological assessment at 27Martins Lane, Dorchester* (Oxford Archaeology (unpublished client report)

Champion, T, and **Collis**, J, 1996 *The Iron Age in Britain and Ireland,* Sheffield: J R Collis Publications

Clark, A, 1997 *Seeing Beneath the Soil: Prospecting Methods in Archaeology,* London: Routledge

Collingwood, R G, 1965 *The Roman inscriptions of Britain Volume I, Inscriptions on stone,* Oxford: Clarendon Press

Collis, J, 2007 "The polities of Gaul, Britain, and Ireland in the Late Iron Age", in (eds C Haselgrove and T Moore) *The later Iron Age in Britain and beyond,* Oxford: Oxbow, 523-8

Cook, J, and **Rowley**, T, 1985 *Dorchester through the ages,* Oxford: University Department for External Studies

Crake, A D, 1874 *Evanus: A tale of the days of Constantine,* Oxford: A R Mowbray and Company

Crake, A D, 1889 *The doomed city, or the last days of* Durocina, Oxford: A R Mowbray and Company

Creighton, J, 2006 *Britannia: the creation of a Roman province,* London: Routledge

Cunliffe, B W, 1986 *The city of Bath,* Gloucester: Sutton

Cunliffe, B W, 2004 *Iron Age Britain,* London: B T Batsford

Cunliffe, B W, 2005 *Iron age communities in Britain: an account of England, Scotland and Wales from the seventh century BC until the Roman conquest (fourth ed),* London: Routledge

Cunliffe, B W, and **Rowley**, T, (eds) 1978 *Lowland Iron Age Communities in Europe,* Oxford: BAR

Cunningham, C J, and **Banks**, J W, 1972"Excavations at Dorchester Abbey, Oxon", *Oxon* **37**, 158-64

Denning, A, 2000 *Dorchester on Thames: status and continuity over the prehistoric and historic periods,* BA dissertation, University of Exeter (unpublished)

Dickinson, T M, 1974 *Cuddesdon and Dorchester-on-Thames: two early saxon 'princely' sites,* Oxford: BAR

Dise, R Jr, 1995 "A reassessment of the functions of *beneficiarii consularis*",*The Ancient History Bulletin,* **9(2)**, 72-85

Dixon, P, 1982 "How Saxon is the Saxon house?", in (ed P J Drury) *Structural reconstruction: approaches to the interpretation of the excavated remains of buildings,* Oxford: BAR

Durham, B, and **Rowley**, T, 1973 "A cemetery site at Queensford Mill, Dorchester" *Oxon* **37**, 32-7

Ekwall, E, 1936 *The concise Oxford dictionary of English place-names,* Oxford:Clarendon Press

Esmonde Cleary, A S, 1989 *The ending of Roman Britain,* London: Batsford

Esmonde Cleary, A S, 2003 "Civil defences in the West under the High Empire", in (ed D Wilson) *The archaeology of Roman towns : studies in honour of John S. Wacher*, Oxford: Oxbow, 72-85

Evans, A, 1893 "Greek and Italian influences in Prae-Roman Britain", *London Times* (September 23), 11

Evans, J, 1881 *The ancient bronze implements, weapons,and ornaments of Great Britain and Ireland*, London: Longmans, Green and Company

Everson, P, and **Knowles**, G C, 1978 "A *tutulus* brooch from Kirmington, Lincolnshire (South Humberside)", *Medieval Archaeology* **22**, 123-5

Fishwick, D, 1961 "The Imperial cult in Roman Britain", *Phoenix* **15(4)** 213-29

Frend, W H C "The Christianisation of Roman Britain" in (eds M W Barley and R P Hanson) *Christianity in Britain, 300-700*, Leicester: University Press 37-49

Frere, S S, 1962 "Excavations at Dorchester on Thames, 1962", *Archaeol J* **119**, 114-49

Frere, S S, 1966 "The end of towns in Roman Britain", in (ed J S Wacher) *The civitas capitals of Roman Britain: papers given at a conference held at the University of Leicester, 13-15 December 1963*, Leicester: University Press, 87-100

Frere, S S, 1967 *Britannia: history of Roman Britain*, London: Routledge and Kegan Paul

Frere, S S, 1984 "Excavations at Dorchester on Thames, 1963", *Archaeol J* **141**, 91-174.

Fulford, M, 2001 "Links with the past: pervasive 'ritual' behaviour in Roman Britain", *Britannia* **32**, 199-218

Fulford, M, 2003, "Silchester: the early development of a civitas capital", in (ed S J Greep) *Roman towns: the Wheeler inheritance*, York: CBA, 16-33

Gelling, M, 1954 *The place-names of Oxfordshire*, Cambridge: University Press

Gibson, A, 1992a, 'Possible timber circles at Dorchester-on-Thames', *Oxford Journal of Archaeology* 11, 85-91

Gibson, A, 1992b The timber circle at Sarn-y-Bryn-Caled, Welshpool, Powys: ritual-and-sacrifice in Bronze Age mid-Wales" *Antiquity* **66**, 84-92

Gibson, E, 1695 *Camden's Britannia, with additions and improvements,* London

Giles, J A, 1872 *Six old English chronicles: of which two are now first translated from the monkish Latin originals,* London: George Bell and Sons

Goodburn, R, and **Waugh**, H, 1983 *The Roman inscriptions of Britain, volume I, inscriptions on stone- epigraphic indexes*, Gloucester: Sutton

Gosden, C and **Lock**, G, 1998 "Prehistoric histories", *World Arch* **30**, 2-12

Gough, R, 1806 *Camden's Britannia, translated and enlarged*, London

Grant, A, 1981 "The animal bones", in Rowley and Brown 1981, 50-5

Hamerow, H, 1995 "Shaping settlements: early medieval communities in Northwest Europe", in (eds J Bintliff and H Hamerow) *Europe between Late Antiquity and the Middle Ages*, BAR International Series 617, Oxford: BAR Publishing, 8-37

Hamerow, H, 1999 "Anglo-Saxon Oxfordshire, 400-700", *Oxon* **64**, 23-38

Harden, D B, and Taylor, M V, 1939 "Romano-British remains", in (ed L Salzman) *The Victoria history of the county of Oxford*, Oxford: University Press, 267-345

Harding, D W, 1972 *The Iron Age in the Upper Thames Basin*, Oxford: Clarendon Press

Harding, D W 1974 *The Iron Age in Lowland Britain*, London: Routledge and Kegan Paul

Hargreaves, G H, Parker, R P F, and Boarder, A W F, 1978 "Dorchester on Thames", *CBA Group 9 Newsletter* **8**, 5

Hartley, B R, 1983 "The enclosure of Romano-British towns in the second century AD", in (eds B R Hartley and J S Wacher) *Rome and her northern provinces: papers presented to Sheppard Frere in honour of his retirement from the Chair of the Archaeology of the Roman Empire, University of Oxford, 1983*, Gloucester: Sutton, 84-95

Haverfield, F, 1895 "A Roman inscription from Cirencester illustrating fourth century Britain" in (ed P Frowde) *Archaeologia Oxoniensia*, 215-26

Haverfield, F, and **MacDonald**, G, 1924 *The Romanization of Roman Britain*, Oxford: Clarendon Press

Hawkes, S C, 1961 "Soldiers and settlers in Britain, fourth to fifth century", *Medieval Archaeology* **5**, 1-41

Hawkes, S C, 1986 "The Early Saxon period", in (eds G Biggs, J Cook, and T Rowley) *The archaeology of the Oxford region*, Oxford: University Department for External Studies 64-108

Hearne, T J, 1711 "An account of some antiquities between Windsor and Oxford", in (ed T Hearne) *The itinerary of John Leland the Antiquary*, volume V, Oxford: Theatre, 127-78

Hearne, T J, 1775 *English Antiquities: a collection of curious discourses written by eminent antiquaries*, London: Ben White

Heighway, C, and **Bryant**, R 1986 "Reconstruction of the 10th century church at St Oswald's, Gloucester", in (eds L Butler and K Morris) *The Anglo-Saxon church: papers on history, architecture, and archaeology in honour of Dr. H. M. Taylor*, London: CBA, 188-95

Henley, Dorchester, and Oxford Turnpike Act, 1735, London

Henig, M, 2002 *The Heirs of King Verica*, Stroud: Tempus

Henig, M, 2007 "Roman Britain," *Microsoft Encarta Online Encyclopaedia* http://au.encarta.msn.com

Henig, M, and **Booth**, P, 2000 *Roman Oxfordshire*, Stroud: Sutton

Hey, G, 2007 "Unravelling the Iron Age landscape of the Upper Thames Valley", in (eds C Haselgrove and T Moore) *The later Iron Age in Britain and beyond*, Oxford: Oxbow 156-72

Higham, N J, 2004 "From sub-Roman Britain to Anglo-Saxon England: debating the insular dark ages", *History Compass* **2**, 1-29

Hill, J D, 1995 "How should we study Iron Age societies and hillforts? A contextual study from Southern England", 45-66 in (eds J D Hill and C G Cumberpatch) *Different Iron Ages: Studies on the Iron Age in temperate Europe*, BAR International Series 602, Oxford: BAR Publishing.

Hill, J D, 2007 "The dynamics of social change in Later Iron Age eastern and southeastern England", in (eds C Haselgrove and T Moore) *The later Iron Age in Britain and beyond*, Oxford: Oxbow, 16-40

Hingley, R, 1983 "Excavations by R A Rutland on an Iron Age site at Wittenham Clumps", *Berkshire Arch J* **70**, 21-55

Hingley, R, 2003 "Recreating coherence without reinventing Romanization", in (eds A D Merryweather and J D W Prag) *Romanization?: proceedings of a post-graduate colloquium, University of London Institute of Classical Studies*, London: Digressus Supplement **1**, 111-19

Hingley, R, 2006 "The deposition of iron objects in Britain during the later prehistoric and Roman periods: contextual analysis and the significance of iron", *Britannia* **37**, 213-57

Hinton, I, 2006 "Church Alignment and Patronal Saint's Days", *Antiq J* **86**, 206-26

Hogg, A H A, and **Stevens**, C E, 1937 "The defences of Roman Dorchester", *Oxon* **2**, 41-73

Horsley, J, 1732 *Britannia Romana*, London

Ireland, S, 1986 *Roman Britain: a sourcebook*, London: Croom Helm

James, S, 2007 "A bloodless past: the pacification of early Iron Age Britain", in (eds C Haselgrove and R Pope) *The earlier Iron Age in Britain and the near continent*, Oxford: Oxbow, 160-73

Jennings, D, **Muir**, J, **Palmer**, S, and **Smith**, A, 2004 *Thornhill Farm, Fairford, Gloucestershire : an Iron Age and Roman pastoral site in the upper Thames Valley*, Oxford: Oxford Archaeology

John Moore Heritage Services, 2002 "12 High Street , Dorchester-on-Thames", (unpublished client report)

John Moore Heritage Services, 2006 "Land adjacent to Chequers, Bridge End, Dorchester, Oxon" (unpublished client report)

Jones, B, and **Mattingly**, D, 1990 *An atlas of Roman Britain*, Oxford: Oxbow

Keevil, G, 2003 "Archaeological investigations in 2001 at the Abbey Church of St Peter and St Paul, Dorchester-on-Thames, Oxfordshire", *Oxon* **68**, 313-362

Kenyon, K M, 1948 *Excavations at the Jewry Wall site,Leicester*, Oxford: University Press

Kirk, J R, and **Leeds**, E T, 1954 "Three early Saxon graves from Dorchester, Oxon", *Oxon* **17-18**, 63-76

Lambrick, G, 1992 "The development of late prehistoric and Roman farming on the Thames gravels" in (eds M Fulford and E Nichols) *Developing landscapes of lowland Britain: the archaeology of the British gravels*, London: Society of Antiquaries, 78-105

Lambrick, G, in press *The Thames through time- the archaeology of the Upper and Middle Thames Valley: the first foundations of modern society in the Thames Valley 1500BC-AD50*

Lambrick, G, and **Allen**, T, 2004 *Gravelly Guy, Stanton Harcourt: the development of a prehistoric and Romano-British community*, Oxford: Oxford Archaeology

Lane Fox, A, 1870 "On the threatened destruction of the British earthworks near Dorchester", *J Ethnological Soc London* (new series) **2**, 412-5

Leeds, E T, 1935 "Recent Iron Age Discoveries in Oxfordshire and North Berkshire", *Antiq J* **15**, 30-41

Lewis, M J T, 1966 *Temples in Roman Britain*, Cambridge: University Press

Limbrey, S, 1975 *Soil science and archaeology*, London: Academic Press

Loveday, R, 1999 "Dorchester on Thames– ritual complex or ritual landscape?", in (eds A Barclay and J Harding) *Pathways and ceremonies : the cursus monuments of Britain and Ireland*, Oxford: Oxbow, 49-66

McCarthy, S, **Nurse**, B, and **Gaimster**, D, (eds) 2007 *Making History: Antiquaries in Britain, 1707-2007*, London: Royal Academy of Arts

MacFarlane, W C, 1881 *A short account of Dorchester, past and present*, Oxford

MacMullen, R, 1963 *Soldier and Civilian in the Later Roman Empire*, Harvard: University Press

MacMullen, R, 1966 *Enemies of the Roman Order*, Harvard: University Press

Manning, W H, 1972 "Ironwork hoards in Iron Age and Roman Britain", Britannia **3**, 224-50

Manning, W H, 1984 "Objects of iron", in Frere 1984, 139-152

Manning, P, and Leeds, E T, 1921 "An archaeological survey of Oxfordshire", *Archaeologia* **71**, 227-65

Mattingly, D, 2006 *An imperial possession: Britain in the Roman Empire: 54 BC – AD 409*, London: Allen Lane Publishers

Miles, D (ed) 1986 *Archaeology at Barton Court Farm, Abingdon, Oxon: an investigation of late Neolithic, Iron Age, Romano-British, and Saxon settlements*, Oxford: Oxford Archaeology and CBA

Millett, M, 1990 *The Romanization of Britain: an essay in archaeological interpretation*, Cambridge: University Press

Millett, M, 1995 "Strategies for Roman small towns", in (ed A E Brown) *Roman small towns in eastern England and beyond*, Oxford: Oxbow, 29-37

Moore, T, 2007 "Life on the edge? Exchange, community and identity in the Late Iron Age of the Severn-Cotswolds", in (eds C Haselgrove and T Moore) *The later Iron Age in Britain and beyond*, Oxford: Oxbow, 41-61

Munby, J, and **Rodwell**, K, 1974 "Dorchester", in (ed K Rodwell) *Historic towns in Oxfordshire*, Oxford: Oxford Archaeological Unit, 101-08

Northover, P, 1992 "Metal analysis", in Whittle *et al* 1992, 194

O'Connor, B, 1980 *Cross-channel relations in the later Bronze Age : relations between Britain, North- Eastern France, and the Low Countries during the later Bronze Age and the early Iron Age, with particular reference to the metalwork*, Oxford: BAR **91**

Oxford Archaeology, 1992 "Watching brief at 1 Samian Way, Dorchester on Thames", (unpublished) client report

Oxford Archaeology, 2007 "Discovering Dorchester" (unpublished training manual)

Pantin, W A, 1939 "The Oxford Architectural and Historical Society, 1839–1939", http://www. oahs.org.uk/oxo/vol%204/Pantin.doc

Parker, A J, 1988 "The birds of Roman Britain", *Oxford J Arch* **7(2)**, 197-226

Parker, J H, 1882 *The History of Dorchester, Oxfordshire and the architectural history of the church*, London: Parker and Company

Parker Pearson, M, **Pollard**, J, **Richards**, C, **Thomas**, J, **Tilley**, C, **Welham**, K, and **Albarella**, U, 2006 "Materializing Stonehenge: The Stonehenge Riverside Project and new discoveries", *J Material Culture* **11**, 227-261

Petts, D, 1998 "Landscape and cultural identity in Roman Britain.", in (eds J Berry and R Laurence) *Cultural Identity in the Roman Empire,* London: Routledge, 79-94

Planning Policy Guidance 16: Archaeology and planning, 1990, London

Pflaum, H G, 1940 *Essai sur le cursus publicus sous le Haut-Empire romain*, Paris

Reece, R, 1980 "Town and country: the end of Roman Britain", *World Arch* **12 (1)**, 77-92

Reece, R, 1983 *My Roman Britain*, Cirencester: Cotswold Studies

Reece, R, 1984 "The hoards", in Frere 1984,132-5

Richmond, I A, 1968 *Hod Hill*, London: British Museum

Rivet, A, 1966 *Town and Country in Roman Britain*, London: Hutchinson University Library

Robinson, M, 1992 "Environmental archaeology of the river gravels: past achievements and future directions", in (eds M Fulford and E Nichols) *Developing landscapes of lowland Britain: the archaeology of the British gravels* London: Society of Antiquaries, 47-62

Robinson, M, 1984 "Landscape and environment in central southern Britain in the Iron Age" in (eds B Cunliffe and D Miles) *Aspects of the Iron age in central southern Britain*, Oxford: University Committee for Archaeology, 1-11

Rodwell, W, 2005 *The Abbey Church of St Peter and St Paul, Dorchester-on-Thames, Oxfordshire: an Archaeological and Historical Survey,* (unpublished)

Roe, D, 1981 *The Lower and Middle Palaeolithic periods in Britain*, London: Routledge and Kegan Paul

Rowley, R T, 1974 "Early Saxon settlement in Dorchester", in (ed R T Rowley) *Anglo-Saxon settlement and landscape*, Oxford: BAR, 42-50

Rowley, T, and **Brown**, L, 1981 "Excavations at Beech House Hotel, Dorchester-on-Thames 1972", *Oxon* **46**, 1-55

Russell, C, 2005 "The Anglo- Saxon influence on Roman Britain: research past and present", *Durham Anthro J* **13(1)**

Salter, H E, 1915 *Remarks and collections of Thomas Hearne volume X*, Oxford: Clarendon Press

Salter, H E, 1907 *Remarks and collections of Thomas Hearne volume VIII*, Oxford: Clarendon Press

Schrijver, P, 2008 "Languages as a key to prehistory: the case of Britain and the Celts", lecture given at the Europa day conference, May 17, 2008: Oxford

Sharples, N, 1991 "Warfare in the Iron Age of Wessex", *Scottish Arch Rev* **8**, 79-89

Stevens, C E, and **Keeney**, G S, 1935 "Ramparts of Dorchester", *Antiquity* **9**, 217-9

Sutton, J , 1966 "Iron Age Hill-Forts and some other Earthworks in Oxfordshire", *Oxon* **31**, 36-60

Swanton, M J, 1973 *A corpus of pagan Anglo-Saxon spearheads*, Oxford: BAR

Taylor, A, 1997 "A Roman child burial with animal figurines and pottery from Godmanchester, Cambridgeshire", *Britannia* **28**, 386-93

Tiller, K, 2005 *Dorchester abbey: church and people 635-2005*, Witney: Stonesfield Press

Todd, M, 1970 "The small towns of Roman Britain", *Britannia* **1**, 114-30

Toynbee, J M C, 1968 "Pagan Motifs and practices in Christian art and ritual in Roman Britain", in (eds M W Barley and R P Hanson) *Christianity in Britain, 300-700*, Leicester: University Press, 175-92

von Domaszewski, A, 1902 "Die Beneficiarierposten und die römischen Strassennetze", *Westdeutsche Zeitschrift für Geschichte und Kunst*, **21**, 158-211

Wacher, J S, 1966 "Earthwork defences of the second century", in (ed J S Wacher) *The civitas capitals of Roman Britain: papers given at a conference held at the University of Leicester,   13-15 December 1963*, Leicester: University Press, 60-69

Watson, G R, 1968 "Christianity in the Roman Army in Britain" (eds M W Barley and R P Hanson) *Christianity in Britain, 300-700*, Leicester: University Press, 51-54

Webster, G, 1966 "Fort and town in early Roman Britain", in (ed J S Wacher) *The civitas capitals of Roman Britain: papers given at a conference held at the University of Leicester, 13-15   December 1963*, Leicester: University Press 31-45

Whittle, A, 1996 *Europe in the Neolithic: the creation of new worlds*, Cambridge: University Press

Whittle, A, **Atkinson**, R J C, **Chambers**, R, and **Thomas**, N, 1992 "Excavations in the Neolithic and Bronze Age complex at Dorchester-on-Thames, Oxfordshire, 1947-1952   and   1981", *Proc Prehist Soc* **58**, 143-201

Wilson, D R, 1965 "Roman Britain in 1964: sites explored", *J Roman Studies* **55**, 199-220

Young, C J, 1977 *The Roman Pottery Industry of the Oxford Region*, Oxford: BAR

www.ingramcontent.com/pod-product-compliance
Lightning Source LLC
Chambersburg PA
CBHW061305270326
41932CB00029B/3478